CW01623381

Pelagia, Edward, Anne and Delphine Garland are all dancers and ballet mad. Their mother is a prima ballerina and their father a conductor of the ballet company orchestra.

Their cousin Joan is an orphan, and has come down from Lancashire to live with the Garlands in London. To begin with she found it hard to fit in and her cousins couldn't understand how she had survived without knowing anything about ballet. But in time Joan discovered her own special talent and outshone them all.

In this second story about the ballet family, everyone has problems to face, not least Anne whose best friend has given up ballet. Joan is presented with a new challenge and she is not sure that she can rise to it ...

By the same author:

The Ballet Family
The Ballet Twins
Ballet for Drina
Drina's Dancing Year

Drina Dances in Exile
Drina Dances in Italy
Drina Dances Again
Drina Dances in New York

The Ballet Family Again

by

Jean Estoril

Macdonald Children's Books

Cover illustration by Anne Eggebert
Black and white illustrations by Beryl Sanders

Text copyright © Mabel Esther Allan 1964
Illustrations copyright © Macdonald Children's Books 1989

First published in Great Britain by
Methuen & Co Ltd

This edition published in 1989 by
Macdonald Children's Books

All characters in this publication are fictitious, and any resemblance to real persons, living or dead, is purely coincidental.

All rights reserved
This book is sold subject to the condition that it shall not, by way of trade or otherwise, be lent, re-sold, hired out, or otherwise circulated without the publisher's prior consent in any form of binding or cover other than that in which it is published and without a similar condition including this condition being imposed on the subsequent purchaser.

Photoset in 11pt Goudy Old Style in North Wales by
Derek Doyle & Associates, Mold, Clwyd

Printed and bound in Great Britain at
The Guernsey Press

Macdonald Children's Books
Simon and Schuster International Group
Wolsey House, Wolsey Road
Hemel Hempstead HP2 4SS

BRITISH LIBRARY CATALOGUING IN PUBLICATION DATA
Estoril, Jean,
The ballet family again.
Rn: Mabel Esther Allan I. Title
823'.914 [J]

ISBN 0-356-16798-4
ISBN 0-356-16799-2 pbk

Contents

Chapter One
New Year's Day

"The worst of it is that you don't care!" said Anne Garland. "I feel so awful about it, and you're quite placid. I believe you're even looking forward to starting a new life."

Though Anne tried hard to control it, her voice was shaking badly by the end of this speech. She gave her friend, Lisa Thorburg, a desperate look, then rose, tossing back her smooth red hair as she walked to the window.

The two girls were in Lisa's room, which her mother had just recently turned into a charming bed-sitting-room. Two comfortable chairs were drawn up in front of the glowing electric fire and they had been very peaceful since lunch until Anne's emotions had got the better of her.

Now she stood at the window, with her back to the room. The Thorburgs lived near Primrose Hill and from Lisa's high window there was normally a wide view of trees and grassy slopes, but on this gloomy winter afternoon the whirling snowflakes were so thick that almost nothing could be seen.

Anne stood there stiffly, swallowing with difficulty, already ashamed of her outburst. She knew that Lisa had risen and was standing behind her, but she could not turn round.

"I'm sorry," she said gruffly. "But you *do* seem to be looking forward to it and I can't get used to the idea that you'll never come back to the Thorburg. That you'll never be a ballet dancer after all."

Lisa's own voice was not quite steady when she spoke.

"Oh, Anne! But you've known for months. October, wasn't it? I know you minded dreadfully then, but I thought you had stopped feeling so badly about it. You haven't even mentioned it for ages."

"That was because so much happened before Christmas. I'd even almost forgotten – except on the very last day of term – that you wouldn't be coming back. There was all that business of Delphine dancing in the competition and being in trouble afterwards, and the Christmas Show and Joan's ballet. Then Helenka coming to us for Christmas when her mother was in hospital. There simply wasn't time to think. But now it's New Year's Day and term starts in a fortnight, and – and things will never be the same without you."

"But you'll have Colin and Fernanda and even Helenka now that you find you like her after all. And we'll still see each other a lot out of school. We *agreed* that it wouldn't make any difference to our friendship."

"I know. Of course you're right; we'll still be friends. I can't imagine anything else. But I can't imagine the Thorburg without you."

They had been friends since the far away day when they had both been new at the Thorburg Ballet School, Lisa the daughter of Johann Thorburg, Director of the School and Ballet Company, and Anne the middle daughter of Mona Garland, prima ballerina of the Company. And the friendship had grown with the years, a satisfying relationship that had never been clouded until Lisa's strange, secretive behaviour at the start of the autumn term. It had been a terrible blow to Anne – and also to

Lisa's father – when Lisa had at last confessed that she didn't want to continue her ballet training. She wanted to go to an ordinary school, she had explained, and maybe specialize in languages as she grew older.

Johann Thorburg had taken it well, for he only wanted his daughter to be happy, but at the time Anne had been inconsolable. It had been pointed out to her by her outspoken family that she was being selfish and only distressing Lisa more than was necessary, and she had then made a great effort to resign herself to the coming changes. But now that the changes were almost upon her....

"You *are* looking forward to the Scott-Smithson, though, aren't you?"

Lisa said slowly:

"Yes, I am. It would be silly not to, since it's what I said I wanted. Of course it will feel strange at first, but I shall know your cousin Joan. Oh, Bunchy, don't spoil it! *Don't* be angry with me!"

The old pet name that had grown out of the fact that Anne was A. Garland was not often used now, and Anne was glad. But spoken in Lisa's soft voice it moved her, bringing back memories of the days when she had believed that she and Lisa would go on together to be dancers in the Thorburg Company.

"I'm not angry. I've said I'm sorry. I'm a selfish beast. But it's only because I shall miss you so much. Joan has promised that she'll look after you when you go to the Scott-Smithson, but of course she has her Peigi – Margaret MacAllister. They're inseparable." Then she looked out at the falling snow and added hastily: "I'd better go before it gets really dark. Mother will only worry. The snow was deep this morning and it'll be worse now. I can't get used to London like this, all smothered in whiteness since Boxing Day. It seems like a strange new world."

They went downstairs and, as they reached the hall, the

front door opened and Lisa's brother Jocheli came in. He was covered with snow.

"Hullo, Anne! It's getting really bad. Rather fun in a way; there's hardly any traffic. Are you going home now? I'd better go with you." Jocheli was a tall boy of nearly sixteen; he was not a prospective dancer, but attended a Grammar School.

"Oh, don't bother, thanks. I'll be all right," said Anne, struggling into her outdoor clothes and bending down to zip up her lined boots. "I like it, too. I always enjoy it when things are unusual. Fog, and terrific heat waves, and –"

"It's certainly not a heat wave now. It's bitter."

Anne dropped her slippers into a little holdall and went to find Mrs Thorburg, to say goodbye. As she opened the door of the living-room she stifled a yawn and Mrs Thorburg laughed.

"It's being up so late that does it. If you will see the New Year in –"

Anne grinned. She had recovered her assurance, at least, though her heart was still heavy.

"Delph was wild because she had to go to bed at ten. But it was really a grown-up party. Joan and Edward and I were so busy handing drinks and things that Mother said we could stay. I didn't get up till nine this morning."

"Well, you'd better hurry home now. Are you sure you'll be all right? Jocheli –"

"He offered. I'll be fine, honestly."

Lisa was waiting by the front door, looking grave and rather pale. She was thirteen, almost exactly the same age as Anne, with brown hair and normally a healthy pink complexion.

"Goodbye, Anne. Don't be miserable. It will all work out."

"Yes, I suppose so. I'd better make a New Year's resolution not to be a selfish pig. 'Bye, Lisa!"

Anne went down the snow-covered steps and turned south towards Prince Albert Road. It was not nearly so dark outside as she had expected. It was, in fact, not much after three o'clock, but the sky was heavy with snow clouds and the flakes were certainly very thick, whirling coldly into her face.

She crossed the road and walked along for some distance with Regent's Park on her left, then, when she came to a gate, she crossed the canal and ventured boldly into the park. Anne was a Londoner born and bred and had been accustomed to going about by herself since she was very young. The fact that the park looked a strange white wilderness – what she could see of it – did not deter her, though her mother would undoubtedly have said that she ought to have returned home by road.

She felt that she needed complete solitude to get her thoughts in order, and on that strange wintry day Regent's Park might have been the remote heart of the country. There were a few people about, mostly young people enjoying snow-fights, but she plodded on with her head bent, ignoring them.

Perhaps it was partly tiredness that was making her feel so unusually depressed, she told herself. New Year's Day ought to be an exciting time of hope and plans. A new year ahead, when all kinds of wonderful things might happen, and all she was feeling was a kind of dull sadness, a most surprising lack of enthusiasm for what lay ahead. Well, what *did* lie ahead was the Thorburg without Lisa, but of course there would be plenty of other things. Visits to Covent Garden, the Royal Festival Hall and the Thorburg Theatre … parties … a chance to read all her new books before term started.

Anne had sometimes said that she could walk around Regent's Park blindfolded, and the obscuring mist of snow was no real deterrent. She went on quite rapidly, making unerringly for one end of the lake, and suddenly it was in front of her; dim and strange, the water near the shore frozen hard.

"Like a setting for a ballet," thought Anne, who always pictured things in terms of the theatre. It was something that had annoyed and bewildered Joan Bradshaw when she had come from Lancashire to live with her Garland cousins the previous September. It had seemed to her that they thought of nothing else, and this was to some extent true. In a household where almost every member was something to do with ballet – Mr Garland conductor of the Thorburg Orchestra, his wife a ballerina, the eldest girl, Pelagia, in the *corps de ballet* and the three younger ones training to be dancers – this was really inevitable. The ways of the family were entirely dependent on classes, rehearsals and performances, and Anne certainly took it for granted.

There were people on the shore of the lake, in spite of the fact that the snow was growing thicker, if that were possible. Some children ran shrieking past, accompanied by a huge and obviously delighted Alsatian ... a crowd of boys were fooling on the edge of the ice.

The Alsatian was lucky, thought Anne. It had long legs, whereas the Garland's black poodle, Bonne-Bouche, was a little frightened of the deep snow.

Then she stiffened, for she had recognized a figure in front of her. There was no mistaking that confident walk and the heavy fawn duffle coat and green Thorburg scarf. It was her brother Edward walking along with a girl; a girl in a scarlet raincoat, with a hood to match.

Edward, who never seemed to bother with girls! Who, in fact, often said that he saw quite enough of women at home.

Anne slackened her pace slightly out of deference to Edward's feelings, though she was dying to know who the girl was. Presently the pair in front turned away from the lake and walked briskly towards the Outer Circle. Anne still followed, wondering if Edward was taking his girlfriend home, but they walked off towards Baker Street, Edward now holding his companion's hand. Once she slipped in the snow and he put his arm round her. They seemed to be laughing.

Well, after all Edward had had his fifteenth birthday just after Christmas, and in many ways he was very adult for his age. Girlfriends had been bound to come. Speculating about her brother took Anne's thoughts away from her own troubles.

Moone Crescent looked dim and curiously unfamiliar in the snow. It was now growing fairly dark and, in spite of her warmly lined gloves, Anne's fingers were cold. She was glad when she reached her home, with its scarlet front door. The little trees in tubs on either side of the steps were almost lost under billowing whiteness. The world seemed unusually silent.

All the Garlands had door keys, because Annali, their elderly Swiss housekeeper, said it was more trouble than it was worth to be letting people in all day long and half the night. Even Delphine (who certainly wasn't out "half the night") had had her own key since she was ten and started at the Thorburg.

Anne fumbled in her pocket and then thrust the key into the lock. She stepped thankfully into the elegant white and scarlet hall, where the air was warm and smelt faintly of newly baked cakes. Very loud music came from the living-room, which probably meant that Pelagia was back from the rehearsal. Fancy a rehearsal on New Year's Day, when most people had been up until one in the morning!

Anne stood shaking her wet gloves and scarf and after a moment identified the music: Arnold's Second Symphony. Then it *was* Pelagia. She was crazy about modern composers, particularly Malcolm Arnold.

Anne took off her coat and was shaking it when the door of her father's study opened and her cousin Joan came out. Joan was the same age as Anne, a tall, thin girl with dark hair, and at first she and Anne had not got on very well together. But Joan had gradually settled down in the Garland household and the fact that she had actually found that she could have a place in their ballet world had helped. For Joan had planned the music, costumes, scenery and story of a little ballet that had been performed by the Thorburg students at the Christmas Show. Joan had seemed very happy lately, so it was strange to see her looking so pale and tight-lipped.

"What on earth's the matter?"

Joan shut the study door carefully and made for the stairs. Stopping on the third step she turned and looked down at Anne.

"I've been talking to Uncle Edwin. I want to go to Lancashire for a few days and he – he says I shouldn't."

"To Lancashire?" The remote village of Wardle on the edge of the moors near Rochdale where Joan had lived had always sounded most unappealing to city-loving Anne. "To stay with your mother's friend, Mrs Thwaite, you mean? I know you always said you wanted to go back some time –"

"I *counted* on going these holidays. I've even saved up most of the fare from my pocket-money and Christmas presents."

"But why doesn't Father want you to go? Because of the weather? We don't usually bother much about weather, with touring and all that. You get used to getting to places somehow." It was a long time since Anne had seen Joan looking so strained and upset.

"Not the weather, though he says it would be awkward if I got snowed up. I'd get out somehow," said Joan impatiently. "I don't mind snow on the hills. No, he – he says he thinks I ought to wait until spring or summer. He –

he says I'll find I've grown away from people there and it will upset me. And it isn't true. I never could. Why, I *lived* there all my life. I belong there. I love London now, but the North is still home in – in most ways. He's left it to me, anyway. He says it's up to me. So I shall go." And Joan turned and raced upstairs.

She was pulled up short, however, by the appearance of Delphine at the top of the stairs, an extraordinary vision. Her small face was heavily made up, her red curls were piled high, and she wore a trailing evening dress and a shawl.

Anne, catching a glimpse of this apparition behind Joan, shrieked with horror.

"Delph! You'll get flayed! Go and take it all off at once! Where's Mother? Isn't she at home?"

Delphine postured, hitching the too-long dress and then clutching the shawl round her narrow shoulders.

"She's been in the kitchen for hours discussing a dinner party with Annali. I was bored, so I thought I'd see what I'll look like when I'm the second Pavlova. What's the matter, Joan?"

Joan had pushed unceremoniously past her.

"Nothing. You gave me a fright, that's all. I'm going up to my room. You'll get shot if your mother sees you."

"You certainly will," Anne agreed. "Second Pavlova or not! That's Mother's new silk shawl, and if you're not careful you'll put your foot through that dress."

"I won't, I'm never clumsy. And I *want* Mother to see me. She sent me to bed last night like a baby, but now I look at least twenty."

Anne gave it up, flung her wet coat on a chair and marched into the living-room, where the Arnold symphony was just coming to an end. Pelagia was lying on the sofa, an inert figure in black jeans and a huge polo-neck orange sweater once sported by Edward, but discarded as too vivid. Her red hair was tied back with a bootlace and she looked anything but the ethereal figure she could be on the stage. She was balancing a box of chocolates on her chest and, as Anne appeared and the record faded into silence, she selected one.

"Oh, hullo!" said Anne. "What time did you get in? Did the rehearsal last ages?"

"Long enough. It was brutal. The theatre was ice-cold and half the *corps* swear they'll die of pneumonia. Something had gone wrong with the heating, but they think it'll be OK by tonight. That didn't help us, though. I've just sneezed three times." Pelagia looked so dismal that Anne stared at her for several moments before flopping down in her favourite chair and starting to pull off her boots.

"It's New Year's Day and it doesn't feel a bit *hopeful.* I almost had a quarrel with Lisa, and Joan looks awfully upset because she wants to go to Lancashire and Father has said better not. And Delph is dressed up in Mother's things. I suppose I ought to *make* her get out of them, but I'm wet and cold. And *you* look terribly miserable!"

"Not miserable, just fed up," said Pelagia, munching another chocolate. "I half-quarrelled with Tim last night."

"Oh! I thought you must have had a lovely time. He took you out to dinner and then dancing. What did you half-quarrel about?"

"Oh, the usual thing. He proposed to me again, and I said I wasn't going to marry for at least ten years. I told him that my life was dedicated to ballet," said Pelagia soulfully, but with a faint glint in her eyes.

"You've told him that before and he doesn't believe you. I really don't see why you shouldn't marry young. Mother did," said Anne. "He's awfully nice. You won't find anyone nicer."

"He's all right. Yes, he is nice and useful for taking me around. But he bothers so."

"He loves you," remarked Anne, who had been much impressed by Timothy Blanford's devotion to the moody and dedicated Pelagia. Of course she was lovely to look at, even in the bulging sweater, with her hair tied up with a bootlace, and simply enchanting when she made a real effort, but she had certainly not given him much encouragement.

"I haven't time for love," her sister retorted. "Good heavens! I'm only in the *corps* and there doesn't seem the slightest chance of a solo role yet. I've got to work and not listen to starry-eyed young men."

"He's nearly twenty-three. He knows what he wants."

"Unlikely to get it," said Pelagia, through a mouthful of soft centre.

"Edward's got a girlfriend. Did you know?"

"No, I did *not*!" cried Pelagia, startled. "Ed doesn't talk about himself and – well, dash it all! He's only fifteen."

"More like seventeen in many ways. Perhaps she isn't a girlfriend, but they were holding hands walking through the snow."

"Who on earth was it? Someone from the Thorburg?"

"I don't know. I only saw her back. Red raincoat and a hood to match. I –"

The door burst open and their mother appeared, pulling a protesting Delphine after her.

"Anne, Delph says you knew she wearing my clothes. I really do think you might deal with her when I'm busy."

"I can't deal with Delph when she's in that mood," said Anne, rather crossly. "Besides, I was frozen stiff and –"

"You've left your boots on the carpet and the dirty snow has melted. Annali will have a fit. Take them away, do, and ask Rosa for a cloth. I *hate* New Year's Day!" said Mona Garland irritably and that made Anne laugh.

"I've been feeling just the same."

"You went to bed too late. Anyway, I hope you've all

made some good resolutions. Delph, don't stand there pulling silly faces. Go upstairs at once and take those things off. And wash your face. You look absurd."

"I've made *one* resolution and that's all I'm making," said Anne. "I always break them."

"And what's that?"

"Not to be a selfish pig," said Anne cryptically and went out of the room.

Chapter Two
Family Life

Joan went slowly up to her room at the top of the tall, narrow house. The only other room on that floor was the studio, where all the Garlands practised. In spite of the intense cold outside the house was very warm, because of the central heating.

She did not turn on the light when she had shut the door behind her, but crossed to the window and stood there, staring out at the falling snow. It was almost dark now and she could only see the dim white outlines of roof-tops and garden walls. But her thoughts were far from the London scene that had grown so familiar. In imagination she was back in the little stone house under the bleak, bare moors where she had lived with her mother. It had been a shabby little house and very cold indeed in winter, but it had been home, and, in spite of all that had happened to her since she was orphaned in early September, she had kept a picture of it at the very back of her mind.

Mrs Thwaite still lived next door and Joan knew that she would be welcome at any time. She only had to write and that would be that. Merely a train journey to Manchester or Rochdale and a short bus ride and she would tread the old cobbled roads again, hear Lancashire voices, and be wrapped in the warm friendliness of home.

Once a journey of more than two hundred miles would have seemed to her very adventurous, but living with the Garlands had definitely altered her views on many things.

The Garlands took travel so much for granted; they journeyed about England with the casualness born of endless touring, and other countries did not seem distant to them. Even Anne and Delphine had, at different times, visited Italy, France, Germany and Holland. So merely going to Lancashire was not much of an undertaking to them and Edwin Garland had mentioned that, in fact, he had to visit Manchester himself on Monday of the following week, as he was appearing on the panel of a television quiz game. He had said that Joan could travel north on Friday and meet him in Manchester on Tuesday morning, but he had most definitely advised her not to go.

Joan was fond of her uncle and trusted his good judgement over most things, but he was wrong this time. Of course he was afraid of her being unsettled, but she knew that it would unsettle her even more to keep the dream of the North Country and not go in reality.

The North Country! Not the beauties of the Yorkshire dales, the wild loveliness of Teesdale or the mountains and water of the Lake District, but the grim country of South Lancashire, where ugly towns jostled each other and harsh buildings rose in stark friezes against the curves of the moors. But to Joan it had always had its own beauty, and her happiest hours had been spent on the moors that were as lonely as anywhere in Britain. Often in those first terrible weeks in London she had thought she would die of nostalgia for the smell of the hills and the sound of the wind in the moor grass. She had described it all often to her friend Margaret MacAllister, who, an exile herself from an island in the Outer Hebrides, had understood better than anyone.

Just by stepping into a train at a London terminus she could have it all again. Not her mother, not her own home, but much that had made her old life happy.

Mother! thought Joan, and for a moment the old pain engulfed her. But she didn't want to forget her mother and it would be good to talk over the old days with Mrs Thwaite and some of her other friends.

After a quite a long time she switched on the light and drew the pretty yellow curtains. Then she stood in front of her favourite picture, a little Lowry print called *The Pond.* Anne certainly thought of Lancashire as "darkest England", but she liked the picture, too. It was she who had told Joan that the picture was in the Tate Gallery and Joan had seen it several times.

Then she got out her writing materials and began a letter to Mrs Thwaite. She owed her one, in any case, to thank her for her Christmas present, and once she had started there was plenty to say, though she was aware that much of it would be Greek to the woman who only rarely went as far as Manchester.

"I hope it will be all right," she ended. "I know it's short notice, but I want to come north for a long week-end on Friday. Uncle Edwin will be in Manchester next Monday, for a northern television programme, and he says I can travel home with him on Tuesday. He says if I am going I had better go now, as he is sure it is going to be a really bad winter. If it isn't convenient could you telephone me please? Otherwise I'll come." And she went on to give train times, for there were always timetables in the hall and that was another thing Joan had learned. She could now look up trains as well as anyone in the household.

Then she stamped the letter and went to put on her outdoor clothes and boots. Edwin Garland emerged from his study just as she was leaving.

"Where are you off to, Joan? The weather seems very bad

now. We shall have to start early for the theatre."

Joan waved the letter a trifle guiltily.

"Only to the post. I've written to Mrs Thwaite. I – I've *got* to go. I'd really like to stay longer, but I've said until next Tuesday."

Her uncle sighed and then smiled.

"All right. You do as you think best. You deserve a holiday after all your hard work. But I wish you'd wait till spring."

But spring seemed unbelievably far away as Joan walked to the end of the crescent. Dropping the letter in the box she felt better, but still a little guilty. Uncle Edwin had been so kind; it seemed ungracious not to heed his advice. But the thing was done now and she was confident that Mrs Thwaite would be ready to welcome her.

On the evenings when any of the older members of the family had to be at the Thorburg Theatre at seven o'clock there was sometimes high tea for everyone about five-thirty, and that evening Edwin Garland was conducting and Mona Garland and Pelagia were both dancing.

During the meal there was the usual slight tension that always preceded a performance, but Joan was used to it now and took it absolutely for granted. Her aunt never talked much on these occasions, but Pelagia was often just the opposite, chattering more than normally.

Delphine was still in an annoying mood, showing off and insisting on feeding Bonne-Bouche from the table, and in the end her mother said sharply. "Will you please behave, Delph? Or perhaps you'd prefer to leave the table?"

Delphine glowered, flicking her long lashes.

"Poor Bonne's hungry."

"He is *not* hungry and I don't want him encouraged in bad habits. Besides, can't you see that we're worried about getting to the theatre?"

"You'd get there if there was an earthquake," said

Delphine, with some truth.

"That may be, but the roads are very bad. Probably it will be a poor audience, for people will be afraid of not getting home. We're fully booked, of course, for *Coppelia* is always popular, especially at holiday times, but still –"

"Some day *I* shall dance Swanilda," said Delphine complacently. "And everyone will say I'm the best there's ever been. Even better than you, Mother."

"*That's* some way off," Anne remarked. She had been very silent so far.

"I'm ten. I shall be in the Company when I'm seventeen, and I expect I'll get my first solo role almost at once. Say nineteen or twenty for Swanilda. It isn't so very long, so you needn't be so crushing, Anne."

"Meanwhile you're an unimportant junior at the Thorburg School," said Pelagia nastily.

"That's just because they don't appreciate me. It was sheer jealousy that they didn't give me a part in the Christmas Show. One of these days they'll *realize* –"

"Oh, skip it!" cried her brother. "You are the worst little show-off there's ever been."

"Everyone's very *cross* tonight," said Delphine, suddenly smiling winningly round the table.

"Well, we don't mean to be," answered her mother, smiling in her turn. Mona Garland could never resist her youngest child when she turned on the charm, though she had few illusions about Delphine. She undoubtedly had character faults that were distressing and even very worrying. Last term she had been in a good deal of trouble at the Thorburg School, and it was to be hoped that she would soon settle down and grow less bumptious and aggressive. "But you know how it is before a performance, and we really are worried about the weather."

In the silence that followed, Pelagia, glanced across at Edward and then said, "Who's the girlfriend, Ed?"

Edward, a very handsome boy with a normally quiet and assured manner, blushed fierily and dropped his fork.

"Oh, Pel, you idiot!" Anne murmured, giving her sister an angry glance. Pelagia was never noted for her tact.

"And who one earth told you that I had a girlfriend?"

"Saw you in the park," Anne mumbled. "I was coming home from Lisa's. You were both walking along by the lake."

"In a *snowstorm?*" asked Edwin Garland, amused and intrigued, but trying not to show it. His son was old for his age, but there had so far been no indication that he was interested in girls.

Edward, still red, retrieved his fork, wiped it, and said curtly, "If you must know we'd been to Madame Tussaud's and then we thought we'd just take a look at the lake."

"To Madame Tussaud's? What on earth for?" Pelagia demanded. "You went a hundred times when you were young."

"Well, where can one go in weather like this? It was somewhere warm and dry where we could talk."

"I can think of somewhere more cheerful than the Chamber of Horrors to take a girlfriend, but I see your point." Pelagia helped herself liberally to a second helping of pudding. All ballet dancers have prodigious appetites and the slender and ethereal Pelagia could eat a whole box of chocolates between meals and still be hungry.

"In any case, it's no one's business but my own," said Edward touchily.

"Granted. But, since we know so much, mayn't we know who the girl is? Someone from the Thorburg?"

"No one from the Thorburg. You wouldn't know her. Her name's Tarn Marlow."

"Good heavens!" cried his mother. "That would look wonderful on a programme. What a waste!"

Edward finished his pudding and rose.

"If you're all going to be facetious –"

"No, honestly we aren't. We're naturally interested."

"Anyway, I have things to do." And Edward marched away, shutting the door firmly behind him.

"Tact will never be Pel's middle name," Anne remarked. "I didn't think she'd blurt it out at the table, in front of everyone. Poor Ed! Now he's upset."

"Yes, I'm sorry," agreed her mother. "But he couldn't have kept it dark for long. I wonder what she's like?"

"I know her," Joan said suddenly. She had been jerked out of thoughts of her coming trip by the family exchange.

"You do?" Everyone, including Delphine, turned to her at once.

"I've never spoken to her. She's at the Scott-Smithson, two forms above me."

"What's she like? Pretty? Intelligent?"

Joan pondered, not wanting to worry her uncle and aunt.

"She's very pretty. Silvery hair and blue eyes. I suppose she's quite good at lessons, since she's in the right form for her age. I think she's fifteen. But –"

"Don't you like her?" Pelagia asked bluntly.

"I've told you. I don't know her. But I've heard things and seen things ... She's rather shallow and silly. Rich, I think; she's the granddaughter of Lord Owlswick." There had been a time when Joan would have been impressed and also irritated by a title, for she had counted herself an ordinary, hard up girl and had gone to the Scott-Smithson School ready to dislike being amongst the rich and pampered. But she had already learned to take their presence for granted. It didn't matter either way, though, by all that she had heard, Tarn Marlow often brought her grandfather into the conversation.

"Lord Owlswick, the wealthy industrialist? If she's really shallow and silly I hope Edward doesn't get hurt," said Mona Garland.

"Nothing we can do about it," her husband pointed out.

"I know. He has to go his own way. But I could wish he'd found a nice, sensible girl for a start."

"Joan has funny ideas," Delphine chipped in and it was Joan's turn to blush.

"If you mean Northern common sense that may be true. But she isn't popular. Oh, well, I wish I'd said nothing." And Joan was glad when the meal was over and those who had to go to the theatre were putting on their outdoor clothes.

Pelagia, in an old duffle coat of Edward's and with a scarf tied over her hair, looked anything but glamorous, but Mona Garland wore her imitation fur coat and a little hat to match.

Meeting Joan in the hall she said, "See that Anne and Delph go to bed early, if you can. They're both tired and Anne doesn't seem quite herself. Edwin says you're going up to Lancashire."

"Just for a long weekend. Do you – mind?"

"Of course not, dear. You're old enough to know what you want to do, and your friends up there will be glad to see you. We'll miss you, though. You're really part of the family now." Mona Garland kissed her lightly and Joan smelt her familiar scent.

The cold air came in as the party streamed down the snowy steps. Edwin Garland had already fetched the car and snow was hiding the pale green paintwork.

"Goodbye!" Anne shouted. "Wish we were coming!"

"You go to bed early, you lucky girl!" her mother called back.

Joan, Anne and Delphine trailed into the living-room, with Bonne-Bouche capering at Anne's heels. Joan was still remembering her aunt's words, with a warm feeling at her heart. They were true, she knew, though once she had never believed that she could be part of the family. The

Garlands' world was now her world, even if she still remembered and sometimes longed for a Northern village.

She plumped herself down in a comfortable chair and Delphine switched on the television. When Edward came quietly into the room they were all absorbed in a serial.

Chapter Three
Joan Goes North

The snow had stopped the next morning, but there was a heavy frost and the sky was still dark. The white and unusually silent streets seemed strange and fascinating when Anne and Joan went to do the shopping for Annali.

"There'll be skating very soon," Anne remarked wistfully. "You'll be all right. *You* don't need to bother about sprained ankles and so on."

"I can skate," Joan admitted. "But I haven't any skates of my own."

"Oh, you can borrow mine or Father will buy you some."

"But don't you really dare to skate?"

"Oh, I do sometimes when it's irresistible, but last winter I fell and was off school for ten days and it gave me a fright. Dancing does come first," said Anne, with a sigh. "Lisa will be able to enjoy herself now. I know she's always longed to skate all she likes."

"You mind dreadfully that she's given up dancing, I know," Joan said.

"Yes. But you're one of the people who said I was selfish. I don't want to talk about it."

Joan didn't pursue the subject, for she realized that Anne was very touchy about it. In any case they reached the nearest shops then and she had to give her mind to Annali's list. Annali was apt to say that Joan was the best shopper in the household and, with a reputation like that to keep up, there must be no mistakes.

By the afternoon Joan's thoughts had turned almost completely to her coming journey to Lancashire. No message had come from Mrs Thwaite so she would definitely be going. Joan made a mental note to buy Mrs Thwaite a very nice present and she did so on Thursday morning, braving the intense, almost frightening cold to go down to Selfridge's.

Her uncle had come home on Wednesday with a first-class return ticket, and when Joan had protested that second-class would have done and that she had almost enough money for that he had said cheerfully, "You may as well be comfortable in this bitter weather, and you'll be coming back with me. You'll need that money for presents and incidental expenses."

So Joan bought Mrs Thwaite some fluffy slippers, and small gifts for various other people. By Thursday afternoon her case was packed and she was in a turmoil of carefully hidden excitement. Anne, teasing, called it "Joan's trip to the darkest North", but Joan had smiled. She had done her best to make them understand that Lancashire was not beyond the bounds of civilization, but she doubted if she had succeeded. The Thorburg Company sometimes appeared in Manchester, Liverpool or Newcastle, but Anne had never accompanied her parents to Manchester, and Pelagia – fairly new to the Company – still had a Northern tour to come.

On Thursday Pelagia was the only one who had a rehearsal and she came bursting home in the middle of the afternoon, her cheeks bright with the cold. She brought a surge of icy air into the living-room, where everyone but her father was gathered. She flung her duffle coat and scarf on to the nearest chair and stood there in her jeans and two thick sweaters, the underneath one, just showing, of a brilliant green and the top one scarlet. Pelagia had no feeling that she should not wear red with her flaming hair.

"You'll never guess!"

"What is it?" asked her mother, who was shortly going out to have some new costumes fitted. "You look very worked up."

"Well, wouldn't you be? I've got my first solo role!"

This was greeted with a loud chorus of exclamations, even Joan joining in.

Pelagia waited and then went on: "Yes, it sounds all very fine, but wait till you hear what it is. Oh, I always thought it would be one of the Blue Skaters, or maybe Dawn or Prayer in *Coppelia*. A fairy in *The Sleeping Beauty* or perhaps the waltz in *Sylphides*. I've dreamed of it; longed for it. And now –"

"Well, what have you got?" asked Joan. Once Pelagia's speech would have meant nothing to her, but now she could understand very well the kind of roles her cousin had hoped for.

"Don't say you're the Duck in *Peter* or something?" said Edward.

"Quack! Quack! Not on your life. You know there's going to be an entirely new production of *Casse Noisette*? They haven't done it for ages. Well, Mr Thorburg told me after the rehearsal that they want me to be Little Clara."

This time the chorus was repeated, but Mona Garland said above it, "I knew that, actually. I heard yesterday, but I left Johann to tell you. I thought you'd be delighted."

Pelagia moaned, wrenching her hair out of the tidy knot that she sometimes wore. The bright red strands came tumbling down and she rooted in the pocket of her coat for her beloved bootlace.

"Little Clara! Me! Having to look like a kid of about eight

when I'd fancied myself all soulful as Prayer."

"But," Anne was much impressed, "it's quite a big part. You'll get a dance in the party scene, and in the Thorburg version there's a little dance with the snow-fairies, and at the end you get up from your throne and dance in and out. And you'll take a curtain with Mother – if she's the Sugar Plum Fairy – and with William Royal, as the Nutcracker Prince. And you'll be billed –"

"Take a curtain in my *nightgown*!" wailed Pelagia. "With my hair loose –"

"You *like* it loose. Only you can't wear a bootlace!"

"I want to be a classical dancer. I don't want to be an idiotic kid in a long nightgown, and pantaloons at the party. What will Timothy think? You know he half-lives in the stalls at the Thorburg when I'm dancing –"

"You don't care what he thinks. You've said so often."

"Well, I don't mind him admiring me. Who would? It's only when he bothers me that I get fed up."

"Well, I think you're being very silly," said her mother, rising. "Delphine, go and telephone for a taxi for me, will you? In about five minutes' time. After all, Pel, you're one of the youngest members of the *corps* and you'll make a most appealing Little Clara. I don't remember that there's ever been a red-haired one. I thought it was a wonderful chance to bring you into the limelight."

"Where are the chocolates? I need sustenance! All my dreams are in the dust," said Pelagia dramatically. "When do you suppose I shall be fitted for the nightgown?"

Her unsympathetic family shouted with laughter and Anne said to Joan, "It's lucky you understand us now. Once you'd have thought we were mad, carrying on like this. Tomorrow, when you're on your Northern hillside – or moorside or whatever it is – you'll be able to tell your friends."

Joan laughed, but the words made her heart lurch.

Tomorrow! North through snow-covered, frozen England to a little stone house. Away from any such conversations, certainly. It was almost unbelievable that she would so soon leave the Garland household and go back to her other world.

Edwin Garland had offered to take Joan to Euston in the car, but Anne, Delphine and Margaret MacAllister all wanted to see her off and Anne pointed out that, as Joan only had a small case, the Underground would do.

There had been a little more snow, followed by frost, and the roads were very bad, so Edwin Garland was not really sorry. He slipped an extra couple of notes into Joan's hand, saying: "Yes, you must take it. Have lunch on the train. Take care of yourself, dear, and meet me at the hotel in Manchester about twelve on Tuesday and we'll have lunch before we leave. Just ask for me at the desk and they'll page me. I only hope you don't get snowed up. There's been a lot of snow in the north."

Joan promised to get out of Wardle somehow on Tuesday morning and then they all set off. Margaret was wildly envious of Joan, who was going back to her own place. For Peigi, though rapidly turning into a confirmed Londoner, still thought nostalgically of the beautiful, remote island of South Uist, where she had lived for so many years.

"Some day *I'll* go back," she said in her soft, faintly sing-song voice.

"Oh, you exiles!" Anne mocked.

"Think how you'd feel if you were deprived of London," Joan pointed out, and Anne groaned at the very idea.

"Anyway, you won't be away long. I expect we'll have lots to tell you on Tuesday night. Things are always happening to us."

Euston station was bitterly cold, but the train seemed very warm by contrast and they all saw Joan into a first-class compartment.

"Don't wait," she said, as two business men entered the compartment and settled themselves, taking papers from their briefcases.

"No. It's always silly," Anne agreed. "You start saying absurd things over and over again. Don't forget to watch television on Monday evening. It's a Northern thing, so I don't think *we* can see Father."

"Mrs Thwaite was talking of getting a set when I left. If she hasn't I'll go somewhere else to watch the programme," Joan promised.

"I wish I was coming. I love trains," Delphine cried.

"Ring me up the minute you get home," said Margaret.

When they had gone Joan sank down in her corner and let the feeling of incredulity flow over her. She was very much aware that the Joan Bradshaw, wearing shabby clothes and with a breaking heart, who had come south in September had been a different girl from the one who now travelled alone. Her clothes were different for one thing, for she wore her cosy turquoise-blue coat and cap to match, with good leather gloves and warm, lined boots. On her knee, with the ballet magazines that Anne had provided, was her leather shoulder-bag, a present from her aunt during one of their first shopping expeditions, when she had been shy and rather aggressive.

That other Joan had known nothing about the ballet world. This Joan had, amazingly, created her own ballet and seen it danced on a London stage. This Joan was confident without being aggressive; she had learned to walk around London as though it belonged to her and had done well at an expensive London school. But her heart still seemed to turn over with excitement at the thought of what lay ahead.

So she left frozen, snow-covered London behind and sat alternately reading and dreaming or looking out at the equally white Midlands. When she went to have lunch one of the business men, who shared her table in the crowded restaurant-car, turned out to be quite friendly and told her that he went to Manchester twice a week.

Then, at last, the train had passed Crewe, and Manchester was not far away. Joan had sunk again into dreamy silence by then and she had to hurry to fasten her coat and collect her things.

Mrs Thwaite was on the platform. Joan saw her through the milling crowd, a dumpy little woman in dowdy grey-brown clothes, with a woollen scarf tied firmly over her head. Her worn face didn't lighten into recognition at first, but then she cried delightedly, seizing Joan's free hand and kissing her on the cheek. "Oh, luv! Ee, I didn't recognize you! By gum, tha've grown tall and tha's reet smart. But come on quickly, luv. There's a Rochdale train in five minutes. Better than t'bus all t'way. T'roads are reet bad, but they're still running up to Wardle."

The familiar voice struck many chords of remembrance, and when they hurried into the Rochdale train Lancashire voices were all about her. Mrs Thwaite chattered unceasingly and Joan was glad, because she was dismayed to find that she was shy and a little tongue-tied.

The train rushed away through the grim scene of warehouses, tenement blocks and frozen canals, and in less than a quarter of an hour was approaching Rochdale. Now there were fields, another frozen canal, red brick buildings in the distance, and, most heartening of all, the sight of the moors in the fading snow-light.

"I've missed it all so much," Joan said, as, on the last stage of the journey, the bus carried them towards the village under the moors. But she was startled and ashamed to realize that now she was seeing the scene as a stranger, and she wondered what Anne would make of the ugly rows of terraced houses, brightened here and there by coloured front doors or a few plants in a window in front of respectably tight lace curtains.

But Wardle was different, for most of the houses were built of blackened stone and had their own harsh beauty. They, like the often abandoned farmhouses on the moors, seemed to have grown naturally out of the countryside.

"Ee, it's Joan Bradshaw!" cried a woman with a market-basket and headscarf, as they left the bus. "Well, I never! I never expected to see thee again, lass. London tha went to, didn't tha? An' how d'you find t'big city?"

"Oh, it's fine," said Joan.

"Sooner thee than me. There's nowt like the North. I were born an' bred here an' pra-ad of it! But tha've turned into a reet smart lass."

A few steps further on they came face to face with a girl whom Joan had known very well. She and Sarah Thorpe had attended the same Grammar School down in Rochdale.

"Hullo, Joan!" cried Sarah, staring avidly at the blue coat and cap. "Mrs Thwaite told me you were coming. Ee, it's grand to see you again. Come to tea tomorrow."

"I'd love to. Thank you, Sarah," said Joan.

She and Mrs Thwaite took the narrow moor road that had once been the most familiar stretch on earth. Now the old worn cobblestones were covered deeply with snow and the biting air stung their faces. The blackened stone walls were topped with billowing whiteness, and, in the rapidly fading light, Joan could see one of the lonely farms perched on the crest of the nearest moor. No lights showed, because it had been empty for a long time. Often, in summer, she had sat on the grass in front of its gaping door with the date-stone over the lintel.

Mrs Thwaite lived in the last row of cottages before the lane went on to the hills. There were lights in the front windows of the house next door and Joan looked at it with less pain than she had expected. That upper room had been hers for a number of years.

"Nice folks they are," said Mrs Thwaite, as she fitted her key in the lock. "Used to live down in Littleborough. There's a lass who goes to tha old school, luv. Ee, I bet tha'll be reet glad of a cup of tea. T'fire's kept in fine and t'kettle's just ready to boil. Make thasel' at home. By gum, my feet are fine and wet!"

And Joan felt ashamed of her high, warm boots when she looked down at Mrs Thwaite's cracked shoes, dark and wet with snow.

"I'll just take thee up, luv. You remember t'room? T'one you had when your poor ma –" Then she stopped abruptly, looking upset. "Seems long ago," she muttered.

Five minutes later, alone in the tiny room with its shabby, old-fashioned furniture, Joan stood by the window, shivering in the icy air and staring out into the winter gloom. Yes, it did seem a long time ago, all that almost unbearable sorrow. And, because she always tried to be honest with herself, she admitted that perhaps, after all, her uncle had been right.

"But I can't have grown so soft, so luxury loving, that I mind cold and a little hard bed," she thought. But it wasn't only that; she realized sharply that now there was a vast gap between herself and the kindly little woman making tea downstairs.

She was increasingly conscious of this as the evening passed. Mrs Thwaite was anxious, even desperately eager, to hear about her new life, but clearly she understood none of it. Over and over again she exclaimed: "Ee, it sounds reet strange to me!" Then once she cried: "All that dancing and your auntie a woman of nearly forty! Time she give it up, if you ask me. T'aint reet. She has her home to think of."

"Oh, Annali and Rosa look after the house. And you should see Aunt Mona dance. Why, in *Les Sylphides* or *Coppélia* she looks just a young girl. Besides, Ulanova and Markova danced until they were much older than forty."

Mrs Thwaite had bought a television set and Joan glanced towards it.

"Haven't you seen ballet now, Mrs Thwaite?"

"Ee, I only got yon set mebbe three weeks ago. There was one programme – daft, I thought it. Summat called *Petrushka*. Beat me, I can tell thee. Lot of silly capers at a fair."

Joan laughed.

"I don't think Aunt Mona dances in that. Not lately, anyway. It isn't in the Thorburg repertoire."

"And all them Garland kids! A *boy* learning to be a ballet dancer. Fine and sissy, I bet he is."

"No, Edward isn't a bit sissy. He's very big and he's going to be a very athletic dancer."

"Your ma never thought much of ballet –"

"No, she didn't care for it," Joan admitted, remembering how, on her marriage, her mother had given up a promising career as a concert pianist and turned her back gladly on the whole Garland world.

"Had her head screwed on, your ma. But go on, luv. Tell me what yon London house looks like."

Joan talked on, but was glad when Mrs Thwaite switched on the television set to watch a favourite programme. She sat in the shabby old chair by the roaring fire, thinking of the moors outside, and was astonished – and once more ashamed – to find that she was glad she would be returning to London in a few days' time.

Chapter Four
Anne and Lisa at Covent Garden

Yet, in the morning, some of Joan's old happiness was back, for she awoke to brilliant sunshine, striking dazzlingly from the white fields and the high, snow-covered horseshoe of the moors.

After breakfast she borrowed an old mackintosh of Mrs Thwaite's to wear over her coat, because she knew that the wind would be cruel away from the sheltered lane; and, with an apple and some chocolate in her pocket, set off. Up and up over the hard, slippery snow, until she breasted the first steep slope of the hill and looked over the wall at the great frozen sheet of Watergrove Reservoir. Then on, past the curve of the wall, where the date-stones of houses and farms and mills that had long ago disappeared beneath the water were mute witnesses to the valley's more vigorous past.

The snow was deep on the old road that went looping on between more of the blackened, roughly built walls that seemed to her the very symbol of that empty country. The snow was too deep for her to see the even older packhorse way that cut up directly over the moors, nothing now, even in summer, but an occasional smooth stone slab in the encroaching bogs. But she struck up boldly, taking a line to the high ridge of the moors. Brown Wardle, Middle Hill and Hades rose with heart-stopping familiarity under a sky that was now softest, palest blue.

This was what she had longed for, and this, at least, still meant all it had ever done: country of solitude and freedom, where now there were no larks singing and only a few dirty-coated hill sheep. She knew that most of the flock would have been taken lower down before the worst of the snow came. But there were the tracks of small animals and birds and the air was sharp and sweet, as the London air never could be. She breathed it deeply into her lungs and the icy wind, catching her as she reached the crest of the moor, made her gasp and stung brilliant colour into her cheeks.

Looking back she could see, beyond Watergrove, the dark spire of Wardle church and here and there a line of dark buildings in the valley. And she wished that she had Margaret with her, so that they could enjoy the hills and the brilliant light together. It was probably nothing like Peigi's island, but Joan knew that she would have liked it, whereas Anne would not have been at home.

The wind blew away her feeling of guilt, but she was conscious that she did not much want to return to midday dinner with Mrs Thwaite and more of the difficult conversation. For, by breakfast time, Mrs Thwaite had been casting her half-pitying, puzzled glances, clearly wondering how it was that anyone could change so much between September and January.

"How could I help it? How could I?" Joan asked herself, remembering the type of conversation to which she had grown so used. The Garlands talked of anything and everything, including subjects that Mrs Thwaite would definitely have thought "Not quite nice", and it had not taken Joan's lively mind long to realize the great benefit of being with articulate people. With Mrs Thwaite she now had to watch her tongue. It was extremely disconcerting and caused her some pain.

She went on again, making for Hades Hill, leaping a frozen stream. And, far away in the distant valley, she heard a train rushing towards the south.

The midday meal was all that she had expected, but it was better when she went to visit her school friend, Sarah Thorpe. The Thorpes lived in one of the old stone houses in the main street, houses that had rows of mullioned windows on the top floors. It was up there, long ago, that people had worked at the hand-looms.

It was quite a while before Joan and her friend got a chance to talk alone, for, as it was Saturday afternoon, Mr Thorpe was at home, and a younger sister and brother. They surrounded Joan, asking endless questions. She was conscious of a faint note of criticism amidst the curiosity, yet it was, undeniably, rather fun to be the travelled one from the great city of London. Fun, at least, until Joan had time to think about it later and to remember that once they had taken her quite for granted, a frequent visitor who had been one of themselves. Now she had the aura of the incomprehensible, romantic Garlands about her, the faintly suspect glamour of a girl from London, who had been to school there for a whole term and who wore smart city clothes.

"Tha certainly looks a different lass," said Mrs Thorpe. "I never knawed tha was pretty. That blue suits thee fine. But tha means to tell us that your auntie is the mother of a great girl of eighteen and still dances on t'Lunnon stage?"

It was always the same. The women of Wardle who were around forty mostly looked it: plump, comfortable, yet with worn faces. They could hardly conceive of what was undoubtedly the truth: that Mona Garland often looked scarcely older than Pelagia.

An oil-stove had been lighted and left to warm Sarah's room, which was one of those on the top floor with the unusual windows. It was still remarkably cold up there, and once again Joan thought of the luxurious central heating of the house in Moone Crescent, but the two girls wrapped themselves in an old travelling rug and sprawled on the bed, gossiping. And Joan was glad to hear news of all her old friends and the various small excitements that had made up the past term at the Grammar School down in Rochdale.

Family tea – a vast meal of ham, egg and chips, followed by home-made pie – brought Joan into contact with the others again, and, though she had enjoyed herself, she was curiously relieved when she walked out into the iron-cold of the cloudy night. A few flakes of snow were falling as she climbed the lane – would Anne have been afraid of the silence and the solitude? – and it was then that desolation swept over her again, because she knew quite certainly that she had given up for ever her feeling of belonging.

She knew it more certainly the next morning, when she sat beside Mrs Thwaite in church. The hymns were mostly melancholy ones and her thoughts roved far from the rhythm of the service. All around her were familiar or half-familiar faces, mostly of the older people: the men with their good Sunday suits covered with shabby overcoats, the women often sitting slumped, glad to rest, their worn hands clasped in their laps, sometimes round sagging handbags. There were some young people, but not many. Here and there were pretty girls, cheaply but smartly dressed. They worked in shops or textile mills down in Rochdale and would mostly marry early and settle in the North as their parents and grandparents had done.

"And I might have been one of them," Joan said to herself. "Well, no, I'd probably have gone to college and become a teacher. But the chances are that I'd have married some local boy and brought up my children here."

She thought of those dream children again that afternoon, once more high on the moors, seeing with extraordinary clarity red-cheeked boys and girls – four of them – climbing the moor roads. Sturdy, shabby, healthy children who took the Northern winds and the smell of sheep and rough grass for granted, as she had taken them for granted in days past.

It had snowed heavily again in the night, but now the sun was shining brilliantly and her feet ploughed softly through the deep drifts until she reached one of the lonely, abandoned farms. And there she swept the snow off a low wall and sat for a few minutes out of the wind, her eyes dazzled by the glare of that huge, wintry landscape.

Wherever her future children roamed it would almost certainly not be here. They would be little Londoners, most likely; perhaps she would even have a ballet child, a child who grew up in the Garland tradition. On Tuesday morning she would leave this place, perhaps for ever, and go back to her London life. And the very worst of it was that she would return gladly.

Meanwhile, at the house in Moone Crescent, life went on with its usual excitements, strains and pleasures. Delphine, ignoring the danger of sprained ankles, skated throughout the hours of daylight and was less annoying than usual when she was at home. Edward was out a good deal, sometimes with friends from the Thorburg and sometimes (Anne and her mother suspected) with Tarn Marlow. But he didn't mention her again and they were tactfully silent.

Pelagia, dancing at every performance at the end of that week, was tired and rather irritable, and Timothy Blandford, appearing at the house to see her briefly before lunch on the Saturday – and of course being asked to stay for the meal – was gloomy.

"I've scarcely seen you since New Year's Eve. Can't we go

somewhere tomorrow?"

"Where, in this weather?" asked Pelagia, who hated cold weather at the best of times and who found the unusually hard frost and bitter winds difficult to bear.

"We could go to the cinema. There are one or two good films on."

"Well, it would be a rest. I could sleep," said Pelagia ungraciously. Timothy didn't care what she did so long as she was beside him, and he was visited by a delightful vision of Pelagia's red head resting against his shoulder.

"Anyway," Pelagia added, "we're going to that posh affair on Tuesday. I've got a new dress for it. Wait till you see it. I look unbelievably glamorous."

"You look glamorous in anything," said Timothy and meant it. From the moment when he had first seen Pelagia in the Tower of London the previous autumn he had known that she was the only girl he would ever love, and this knowledge had grown and deepened the more he saw of her. He worked in his father's firm in the City and was already doing very well. He could afford to marry, but Pelagia wouldn't even discuss the subject rationally.

Timothy's father, who had met Pelagia and who thought her beautiful but unstable, had tried to advise his son to forget her, or at least admit to himself that Pelagia was unlikely to make anyone a good wife. But Timothy went his own way, suffering mainly in silence, but occasionally against his better judgment, trying to make Pelagia understand. For Timothy had it all worked out and could see no reason why such a marriage shouldn't be a success.

They could find a small, convenient flat not too far from the Thorburg Theatre (he had even looked at one or two that might be suitable near Bloomsbury Square and Great Russell Street), and they would organize their lives so that Pelagia would not be too much worried by household cares. A "treasure" like Annali would probably be difficult to find, yet he even had hopes that Annali, when approached, would know of some sensible Swiss girl who would be glad to work in London.

He would be working by day, and Pelagia often both during the daytime and in the evenings, but there would be Sundays and holidays. She would have to go on tour, of course, but then the so far mythical "treasure" would look after him, and whenever possible he would join his wife. It just had to work out that way, for he had no remotest hope that Pelagia would give up ballet. He didn't even want her to, for there was a strange, slightly painful magic in watching her dance. He had never yet grown used to seeing her as a beautiful, unearthly Sylphide, a peasant girl in *Coppélia* or a skater in *Les Patineurs* and then getting her back afterwards, real and hungry and smelling faintly of greasepaint.

Pelagia without ballet was impossible to imagine, but he could very easily imagine her as a bride. The only trouble was that Pelagia seemed to have no leanings that way.

"Oh, well," thought Timothy, watching his love putting away an enormous lunch, "she's only eighteen. Perhaps I'm expecting too much."

Anne had cheered up a little since New Year's Day and had been to two parties. One had been given by Colin Corbett, a special friend at the Thorburg, and one by another girl at the School, Marris Mayhew. Lisa was asked to both and went looking very attractive. A few people remarked sadly on her coming new life, but on the whole the subject was not mentioned.

Anne had not forgotten that soon she would be going back to the ballet school without Lisa, but meanwhile they were seeing quite a lot of each other and things seemed peaceful between them. The only trouble was that they were both carefully avoiding mentioning ballet, and this was particularly difficult for Anne, as her life hinged on it at every point.

It was therefore hard to know what to do when, late on the Monday afternoon, their next door neighbour, Mrs Jolly, knocked and offered two tickets for the Royal Opera House that evening.

"We're *always* buying tickets and not being able to go," she said sadly. "But my husband has to go up to Glasgow tonight and I haven't even packed for him yet. He'll be late home, too. Still, I know you can always use them."

"It's terribly kind of you. Of course we'll use them," said Anne.

"It's *Persephone, The Firebird* and the *pas de deux* from *Le Corsaire*. And you know who's dancing in the *pas de deux*?" And she named a very famous Russian male dancer.

Anne shut the door on the icy world outside and stood hesitating in the hall with the tickets in her hand. Covent Garden! She had been many times, but there was always a thrill in going to the Opera House and the Jollys always bought such good seats. When Anne went with her friends it was usually a matter of climbing up to the amphitheatre.

The thing was, though, who would go with her? Edward was out and had said something about being out that evening; Pelagia and her mother were dancing; Delphine had been invited to a party.

Lisa – it seemed incredible that Anne had to hesitate before asking Lisa to go to a performance of ballet. Incredible and awful. Not that Lisa had given up seeing ballet when she gave up all thoughts of being a dancer. She had said that she hoped to go often, but since New Year's Day there had been that dreadful feeling that it was safer not to mention it … Anne sighed and turned towards the telephone.

"It's me. It's not Lisa. I've *got* to get used to the idea somehow. I'll ask her."

Lisa, when called to the telephone by Jocheli, agreed with apparent eagerness.

"Of course I'll come, Anne. It's not snowing now" – it had been, quite heavily, earlier in the day – "and it's ages since I was at the Garden. I'll go with Father when he drives to the Thorburg. And you can travel with your people, can't you? Meet you about seven."

"Stalls Circle," said Anne and rang off feeling curiously weak at the knees. Oh, life was dreadful when it produced changes that shook a long-standing relationship.

But in the car, being driven slowly through the white and glittering streets, the undying magic was back. Anne had watched performances of ballet from the wings when she was scarcely old enough to walk, and since then she had seen endless finished and unfinished performances. Rehearsals at all stages of production were a commonplace to her, but there was still a thrill in the rising of any curtain, and most of all at Covent Garden, when the red and gold curtain swished back to reveal the great stage.

"I *do* love it more than the Thorburg!" she cried, as her father brought the car to a standstill among all the taxis and hurrying people in front of the Opera House.

"Heresy or worse!" Edwin Garland said, laughing. "You and Lisa had better come over to the Thorburg afterwards. You don't want to try and get home by Tube. Not all the buses are running and there'll be a huge crowd on the trains."

Anne promised and was borne through the doors into the warmth and light. In spite of the weather plenty of people seemed to have arrived already and the men at the inner doors were just starting to take the tickets. Lisa was there, wearing the red coat that suited her so well, and they walked forward down the familiar passage and then up the side stairs into the auditorium.

"We're grand tonight," said Lisa, as, having bought

programmes and left their coats, they took their seats in the front row of the Stalls Circle. Many of the red plush seats were still empty and she gazed around appreciatively. "There's just nowhere like the Opera House."

"I know. I'm often told it's heresy, though," Anne remarked.

"Well, of course it is. We ought to cleave to the Thorburg," Lisa said, without embarrassment. It was Anne who was conscious of tension and once more she hated herself and Lisa, a little.

"I believe I'm jealous," she thought. "Jealous because she's going to like her new life. I must be the most loathsome girl alive!"

But soon she forgot her troubles, for they both concentrated on their programmes, noting which dancers were dancing the different roles. Lisa had never seen *Persephone*, but Anne had seen it once. There was still a great deal to take in, however, for the French verse, with its translation, was printed in the programme.

"So strange to have speaking in a ballet," said Lisa.

"Oh, but it's been done before, though not, perhaps, by the ballerina. Songs, too. Remember those lovely songs in *La Fête Etrange*?"

"And the commentary in *Peter and the Wolf* and *Alice in Wonderland*. But French verse does seem strange."

"She speaks it beautifully, though. You can hear every word and I was in the amphitheatre before. She wears a tiny hidden microphone."

Then the members of the orchestra took their places and began to tune up and the seats gradually almost filled. Not many people, it seemed, had been put off by the bitterly cold night and the difficulties of getting home.

The Firebird was one of Anne's favourite ballets and she watched it with her usual intense pleasure, carried away by the wonderful movements of the very great dancer in the dance between the terrified Firebird and Ivan Tsarevitch. The Prince took the feather that was later to save him from the terrible Kostchei, a magician, and Anne sank back with a little sigh as the Firebird disappeared, and the twelve enchanted maidens appeared from the castle and began to dance.

Ivan, left alone, decided to follow them, but Kostchei arrived, followed by the horrific characters that always made Anne's spine tingle a little. Soon came the breaking of the great egg that held Kostchei's soul, and the ballet moved on to its end – the end that always seemed to her one of the best moments in ballet, though there was little dancing in it. It was mostly the wonderful Stravinsky music, rising to crescendos of sound, the brilliant backcloth and the colours of the costumes as the procession of princes and princesses formed up. The last few bars ... the moment when the curtain came swishing down in the way it only did at Covent Garden, always left Anne breathless and much moved.

As they went up to the Crush Bar to buy coffee Anne gazed at the chandeliers, the mirrors and the flowers and said suddenly, "How odd for Joan to be on that Lancashire hillside. Just at this moment she ought to be watching Father on television. I wonder if she is."

But her mind could give her no picture of her cousin in the little snowbound house far away, sitting curled up in a sagging old chair and watching her uncle, Edwin Garland, being suave and clever in the Manchester studio.

It was a very odd sensation indeed for Joan to realize that this was the man with whom she sat at table every day, who had helped her with the music for her ballet and whom she would meet the very next morning.

Mrs Thwaite, who had met Edwin Garland when he came north to fetch the orphaned Joan, seemed to find it even more peculiar.

"He's a fine-looking chap and no mistake," she said, at

the end. "But I didn't understand more'n a quarter of what any of them were saying. Too clever by half, if you ask me. Ee, it must be reet queer to live with those Garlands!"

And Joan, who *had* understood and appreciated the programme, smiled and made some vague remark, then sank down into wondering just what her cousins were doing at that very moment.

Anne had soon forgotten Joan again, for the *pas de deux* was splendid and exciting. The elevation of the male dancer brought gasps from some of the people near her, and at the end there was wild applause that went on and on, ringing round the tiers of seats, echoing from the high domed roof.

It was then, as the lights went up, that Anne glanced upwards and clutched Lisa's arm.

"Lisa, look! Up there at the front of the Balcony Stalls!"

"Edward!" cried Lisa. "I don't think he's seen us. He's –"

"He's quite sufficiently absorbed," Anne said drily, for her brother was turning to talk to a girl with silvery hair, who wore a blue dress. They were far away, but there seemed no doubt that it was Edward's girlfriend, Tarn Marlow.

"She *is* pretty," Anne remarked. "But Joan says she's shallow and silly. But then one can't tell with Joan. She's very high-minded."

Lisa made a small, protesting sound.

"She's sensible, that's all. I should think her judgement might be trusted, though it's to be hoped she's wrong for Edward's sake."

"You don't know Joan; not really."

"Well, I've met her quite a few times and I do like her. I'm glad I'm going –" and then Lisa bit back the rest of the remark.

But the slight tension did not last long, for both were looking forward to *Persephone*, and when the house lights dimmed again Anne sat back with a sigh that was mostly one of anticipation. It was no use spoiling the evening because Lisa was going to school with Joan.

And soon she had forgotten everything but the strange spell of the ballet, which, unusually, partly arose from the ballerina's clear, but slightly husky voice speaking the French verse. Persephone in the Underworld, a beautiful, haunting figure and never more so than at the very end, when she returned slowly, slowly to the nether regions wearing a many-coloured, shining cloak.

Once more there was wild applause, flowers, many curtains, and when the house lights went up there were still cheers, with the ballerina smiling, assured, holding one of the bouquets. In those moments Anne was flooded with a sudden, violent longing that some day it might be for her that great audiences lingered and clapped. It would not be enough to have partial success. Anne dreamed of reaching the heights – as almost all ballet students do – but she knew more surely than most people that only one in many hundreds of dancers could achieve greatness and lasting fame.

Anne glanced sideways at Lisa and wondered how her friend could give it all up without a pang: the hope, the excitement, the chance of fame. Yet there was the fear, too – fear of not being good enough, of injury – and Lisa would be free of that. Free, as she wished, to be an ordinary girl, with time to pursue many interests.

"We'll be last out," said Lisa, as they retrieved their coats.

"I don't mind. I love the Opera House when it's empty."

"But they'll be waiting for us. It's late."

They walked out into the bitter air, cut through Broad Court and set off towards Kingsway. It had been a mainly happy evening and a little of the magic remained as they went together through wintry London.

Chapter Five

Anne without Lisa

Joan had to walk out of Wardle on Tuesday morning, as the buses were not reaching the village. But, once on the main road, things were easier and she reached Manchester without difficulty. She was in a strange mood, sad, regretful and still guilty, and her uncle was disturbed by her gravity when they met in the enormous lounge of the hotel.

She was very silent during lunch and during most of the train journey, but he did not try and press her to explain. She did talk about her walks on the snowy hills, about tea with her old school friend and church on Sunday morning, but she did not enlarge on her feelings.

So Edwin Garland read his newspapers and Joan alternately read and looked out of the window as the train sped south. She knew that she ought to be honest and confess that her uncle had been right, but it would be a hard thing to do, a very hard thing to put into words.

It started to snow when they reached Rugby and after that the train went very slowly, stopping often in the white wilderness. In the sudden silences they could hear the howling of the wind. Edwin Garland sighed and smiled and remarked that it was a good thing he was not conducting at the Thorburg that night.

"I remember how I had to rush that time I brought you south in September. But now, thank heaven, it doesn't matter if we are late."

This was certainly just as well, as there were few taxis and they eventually had to make the journey by Tube, trudging against the wind from Baker Street Station to Moone Crescent.

As they approached the house they saw that a taxi was waiting outside and Edwin Garland said, "That can't be for Mona. She isn't dancing tonight, and Pelagia will have gone long ago."

"She's going to that dance at the Dorchester – Pelagia, I mean," Joan remarked.

"Oh, yes, I'd forgotten. Not dancing at the Thorburg tonight. It must be Timothy, then. Efficient boy!"

Timothy was in the living-room when the snow-covered travellers burst in. He was being entertained by Anne and Delphine, and, while the newcomers were still being greeted and questioned, Mona Garland appeared. She kissed her husband and then enveloped Joan in a warm hug, retreating with a little shriek.

"Child, you're soaking! And so cold. Go and get out of those clothes at once. You can tell us all about it afterwards."

But before Joan could move Pelagia entered and even her family gasped. For gone were all the thick sweaters and the bootlace and Pelagia was lovely and ethereal in a filmy white dress, with her shining hair elegantly arranged.

Timothy was speechless when confronted by this vision, but the others all exclaimed, "Pel, you look smashing!"

"Just wonderful! It's a gorgeous dress."

"It will knock the Dorchester for six!"

"I just thought," said Pelagia demurely, "that I'd let you all see me. Now I'm going to pile everything I can find on top. I'm going to borrow Ed's old sheepskin jacket and –"

"Oh, Pel, you *can't*! The cloakroom attendant will have a fit. That jacket is so old it smells –"

"It keeps the cold out, anyway. I'm not going out in this weather half-naked."

"I told you could borrow my imitation mink coat," said her mother. "I'm not going out tonight."

"I didn't think you really meant it. It's nearly new and I couldn't possibly –"

"You can't disgrace Timothy."

Pelagia rushed off and came back in the beautiful coat, childishly delighted by her appearance.

"I feel like a million dollars! OK, Tim, let's go, or someone will have nabbed that precious taxi."

"Not likely," said Timothy, "I tipped the driver pretty well to wait."

They went out together, a handsome young couple, and Mona Garland sighed as the door closed.

"I don't wonder that poor Timothy's besotted with her. She looks lovely tonight."

Annali arrived then and combined greetings with cries of horror at all the snow the travellers had brought in. They began to disperse and Joan ran upstairs with her boots in her hand. The warm, fragrant house was home and it was *good* to be back, good to see her own room again.

But the very fact that she loved it so and all the happenings that surrounded "the ballet family" brought back her sadness and vague feelings of guilt. She felt that it would be a long time before she came to terms with herself after that visit to the North.

"What's the matter with Joan?" Mona Garland asked her husband a few days later. "She's so quiet and withdrawn, almost as she was when she first came to us. Did something happen to upset her when she went north?"

Edwin Garland shook his head.

"I don't know. She seems to have enjoyed some of it, but she wasn't at all forthcoming. I wish she hadn't gone, but there was no stopping her."

"Is she missing it again, do you think? I thought she was so happy in London now."

"I've no idea what she's feeling. She's a reticent girl. She certainly looks rather miserable, or perhaps just thoughtful."

Anne, on being questioned tactfully by her mother, said impatiently, "I don't know, honestly, Mother. Joan doesn't confide in me, though we get on quite well now. It can't surely be that she wishes she still lived in Lancashire? I'm sure she loves London and I believe she likes all of us. She was laughing with Rosa just now."

"Joan and Rosa have always got on well, partly because they were both exiles. Poor Rosa missed the Swiss Alps dreadfully when she first came."

Edwin Garland called Joan into his study one morning and she came defensively. But he didn't attempt to force her confidence even then.

"Look, dear, I'm arranging for you to have extra music lessons at school, from one of the visiting masters, Signor Caroni –"

Joan gasped and colour flooded her cheeks.

"Oh! But he only takes the very top music pupils; the élite. and it would cost an awful lot, even if he'd accept me."

"Don't worry about the money. You must be trained. You're too promising a musician to be wasted. He's accepted you already. I know him slightly and I told him all about your mother teaching you so well. He remembers your mother when she started her musical career; he was one of the people who were sorry when she gave it up. He'll be glad to teach you."

A little of Joan's old manner came back, a touch of stubborn pride.

"But I'm going to be a schoolteacher. I made up my mind long ago. You can't visualize *me* as a concert pianist. I – I just haven't got what it takes."

"Maybe not. But you've some talent and if you're going on with composing ballets musical knowledge will never be wasted. Then there's art. I've also arranged with Miss Smithson for you to have extra lessons. Child, those costumes and that set you designed showed most unusual talent and inventiveness. You'll never turn into a common or garden teacher, whatever you may think. You're a chip off the Garland block. You'll make a name in the theatre unless I'm much mistaken."

Joan was now glowing with pleasure and she looked a different girl from the one who had gone so quietly about the house since Tuesday.

"Do you really think so? I *would* work. It's – it's terribly nice of you." Then, with a burst of difficult candour, "I – I ought to tell you. You were right, and – and I do rather hate myself. Everyone was so kind when I went back to the North, but I – I was a stranger, different, and they knew it and I knew it. I – I missed London and all of you and they didn't know what I was talking about."

Edwin Garland was silent for a few moments, studying her thoughtfully. "You've learned a lot. I was afraid of something like that happening."

"But you wanted me to wait. I'd only have grown *more* different in the interval."

"Well, I just wanted to put it off, because I knew you'd be distressed."

"But Mother loved it. She was happy there. She never found them narrow or missed London at all."

"Your mother was an unusually simple and downright woman," he said, a trifle sadly. "I've never known how a Garland could turn out like that. She was different from all of us, always scornful of our preoccupation with the theatre. She made a Northener of herself and was happy. We can't all be the same. And you ought not to fight what you are. Don't be miserable or feel guilty. It will do no good.

"But if – if Mother had lived I should have stayed there all my life and been a different kind of girl."

"Yes. If – we know how many 'ifs' there are in life. Things have worked out this way for you and you're a true Garland. Don't mind it, dear."

Joan escaped then and soon put on her outdoor clothes and set off towards Sussex Mews, where Margaret MacAllister lived. The wintry weather showed no signs of ending and the Mews was deep under snow. The MacAllisters' house was a charming one in a corner, painted blue and white, with wrought-iron balconies.

Margaret greeted her cheerfully and they retreated to her

little room, which was decorated with many photographs of South Uist. There was also an original painting of a great white shore, with pale green sea changing to indigo in the distance and a red boat in the foreground.

Joan flung herself down and poured out about the music and art lessons and the rest of the conversation with her uncle. Only to Peigi could she say anything that came into her mind, for they understood each other as fully as Anne and Lisa had once done. The friendship had been of immeasurable benefit to both of them in the days when they were lonely and ill-adjusted, and they had much in common.

"When do the others go back to the Thorburg?" Margaret asked presently.

"Monday. Delph is starting to be silly again, saying that they don't appreciate her or are jealous because she has talent. She says she'll make them notice her this term. As though they didn't last term!" Joan said ruefully.

"She was always in trouble, I know. One day they'll throw her out and then everyone will be dreadfully upset."

"They nearly did after the competition business, but it only sobered her for a week or two. I like Delph, but she's a perfect little idiot. I know that Aunt Mona worries, and Anne worries, too, because she has to bother about Delphine."

"Well, Edward is there as well. Can't *he* curb her?"

"Oh, Ed goes his own way. I think he's very grand at the Thorburg, with a lot of friends. I've heard him say that if Delph gets thrown out she's asked for it. And just now he's taking even less notice of us all than usual. Anne saw him at Covent Garden with Tarn Marlow. I told you."

"Tarn Marlow isn't nice. She's just out for a good time. She likes to be admired."

"He'll find out, I suppose," Joan said rather sadly. She liked and admired Edward and would have been glad to see more of him. She certainly didn't want him to be hurt by Tarn Marlow.

"And Anne's Lisa is coming with us. I wonder if she'll like the Scott-Smithson?"

"Well, I should think she will. She asked to go there. We'll have to look after her. I promised we'd take her the first day."

Margaret nodded.

"Of course we'll look after her. I remember what it was like being new. If you hadn't taken me under your wing –"

"Still, we've got another week of holidays after they go back to ballet school."

"And snow, snow, snow!" cried Margaret, wandering to the window and staring at the thick flakes that were starting to fall again. "I can't get used to it. We never had much snow in the Isles. I hate being cold and we were frozen up this morning."

"But it was awfully far north, Peigi. Wasn't it cold there?"

"Not often. Never as cold as this that I remember. It was westerly and often quite warm even in winter. Why, I remember one Christmas Day when Father and I walked for miles along the shore and the sun shone and it was like spring. But there were dreadful gales and a lot of rain. Oh, you must come with me some day. We may go back in early September. Mother said the other day that you could come with us."

"I hope *you* won't feel as I did when I went back to Lancashire."

Margaret sighed.

"I hope so, too. But it must always be beautiful. I miss the sea most dreadfully. Shall I play the record of *Fingal's Cave* that you like? I saw Staffa once from the sea, all brooding and dark, the mouth of the cave quite black."

Joan nodded and she ran to put on the record. They settled down comfortably and let the music pour over them.

Rehearsals for *Casse Noisette* had started and Pelagia was still loud in her dislike of being Little Clara.

"They're putting it on in less than three weeks' time. The new sets are almost ready. How I shall hate sitting there looking starry-eyed and wondering while everyone else dances. Little Clara ought to be a real *child*."

"Well, sometimes she is," said her mother. "But they didn't want to use anyone from the School in term-time. And, whether you like it or not, you'll look young enough."

"That darned nightgown!" groaned Pelagia. "And for one thing it's going to be perishing cold sitting in a blast from the wings for all that time. I shan't look a very starry-eyed Little Clara if I'm blue all over and my teeth are chattering."

"It's one of the penalties of a stage life – draughts from the wings, I mean," said Anne, who would have given almost everything she possessed for the chance to be Little Clara. "Stop moaning, *do*!"

Anne was very dismal during the last days of the holidays and she was not looking forward to Monday morning, even though it would mean being back at work at her usually beloved Thorburg.

At the weekend Mona Garland and Annali held a survey of school uniforms, just to make sure that nothing was missing, and on Sunday evening there was a final arranging of cases, gloves, scarves and boots in the hall.

"Because I know what you're all like," said Mona Garland. "Delph will be shrieking for a lost glove and someone's scarf will have disappeared. Fetch your cloak out of the hall cupboard, Anne. I'm sure I noticed that the lining is torn. Yes, just look at it. Mend it at once, please, or it will only go worse." And Anne, who hated sewing, obeyed gloomily. All the girls at the Thorburg had cloaks, mainly to put on after ballet classes.

"It's like organizing an army," said Delphine, eyeing her little green case affectionately. "And Ed doesn't need organizing. He's always ready in time."

"He's rather a one for staying in bed these cold mornings, though, and we've all got to mend our habits now that the holidays are over. Breakfast had better be especially early in this weather. You'll have a fight to get there, if the buses are erratic and the trains not much better. A lot of the points were frozen up yesterday morning."

"We could really walk all the way without killing ourselves," remarked Edward, who often did.

"Yes, but the pavements aren't too good and it would take longer than usual. I don't think the girls should walk, when they've got a ballet class almost at once. It's too much for them. Just get up when Annali calls you. Next week it will be Joan's turn, too."

"Lucky thing to have another week at home!" said Anne, through the open living-room door, and her mother frowned and sighed. It wasn't like Anne to wish for another week away from the Thorburg. Usually she couldn't get back there quickly enough.

Joan, the next morning, heard the general rumpus – doors banging, taps running. Delphine shouting for something – and turned over luxuriously. It certainly was nice on such a dark and obviously bitter morning – though how delightfully warm her room was! – not to have to throw herself into the maelstrom of the rush hour. Even when she did return to the Scott-Smithson she only had to walk the short distance to Dorset Square.

Delphine ran up the stairs to the top of the house just before leaving. She wore her green Thorburg suit and big coat and her beret was at a jaunty angle.

"'Bye, Joan, you stuffy thing! Mother says breakfast for the rest of you in twenty minutes. Don't you like my hat at this angle?"

"Very fetching!" said Joan, smiling up into the pert, self-satisfied little face.

"I'm pretty, aren't I? Don't you think I'm pretty, Joan? The best looking of all the Garlands."

"*Delphine*!" shouted Anne from far below and Delphine snorted and ran, saying over her shoulder, "I'll be a ballerina yet. You'll see!"

Anne was champing with impatience and some irritation. Her mother had insisted that Delphine must travel with her while the weather was so bad. Edward had already gone, loftily in time, and Anne thought with a surge of sadness that normally Lisa would have walked across the park and would be waiting at the end of the crescent. Perhaps, in this weather, she wouldn't have managed it, but they would have met at the Thorburg. And now Lisa, like Joan, was probably still in bed. Anne wondered how on earth she felt, knowing that the Thorburg would be going on without her.

Her mood did not improve as she and Delphine struggled towards Russell Square. They strap-hung to Piccadilly Circus, where they fought their way on to an even more crowded train. Delphine was annoyingly chatty and showed off to anyone who would listen, and all the time the awareness hung over Anne that Lisa would *not* be at the Thorburg. It would mean someone else in the next desk, someone else with the next peg in the cloakroom, no one who understood things without being told.

The trees were snow-tipped in Russell Square and there was deep snow under them, lying in drifts. A few of the younger boys and girls from the Thorburg were having a snow-fight, but those of Anne's age were too dignified to behave so childishly near the school. Anne spied Colin Corbett and Fernanda Vrego going up the steps and Helenka Koronov came towards her just as Anne reached the bottom of the flight. Delphine had rushed off to join the snowballers, in spite of Anne's protests.

Helenka smiled at Anne very warmly and Anne smiled back.

"Hullo, Helenka. Is your mother quite better now?"

"I guess so, thank you. She needs a vacation, but where could she go in this weather?"

When they were very young Helenka and Anne had been bitter rivals and Anne had been glad when the Koronov family moved to New York. Helenka's return as a grave and much changed girl the previous term had been upsetting for some weeks, and Anne had done her best to avoid her until the night of the Christmas Show, when Helenka's mother had been in hospital and Helenka had been invited to spend Christmas with the Garlands. She had left on New Year's Eve to join friends from America at a hotel, but the time they had spent together had made them realize that now, though perhaps still rivals, they might also be friends.

Anne sniffed the warm air of the Thorburg, but was not visited by her usual surge of thankfulness to be back. But on the way to the cloakroom she met many old friends and did her best to chatter as usual.

Fernada put her coat on the peg next to Anne's, saying "Shall I keep you company, Anne, now that Lisa's gone?"

"If you like," Anne said ungraciously, fumbling with the zips on her boots.

"You miss her, we all realize that. We shall miss her, too. Lisa was always so nice, so kind, so very popular."

Anne didn't answer; she couldn't. It might partly be, she supposed, that she was a creature of habit. Lisa had always been there since their very first day long ago; they had always sat together in the hall during the first assembly, and Lisa was always just in front or behind her at the *barre*. She changed fiercely into her practice costume and, snatching up her cloak, hurried after the others towards the hall.

It wasn't that Anne had no other friends. She, too, had

always been popular with most people, though there were a few who were jealous because the Garlands were so important. That was a difficulty that Anne fully recognized, where Delphine did not, and she had always tried to play safe, never showing off or taking advantage of the fact that Johann Thorburg was a family friend. But Lisa had been that rare person, the one to whom she could speak unthinkingly, as Joan could to Margaret MacAllister. She thought drearily that it would be a long time before anyone could take Lisa's place in just *that* way, and then she realized with a shock that, in fact, she was supposed not to have lost Lisa at all.

"I'm thinking about her as though she were *dead*," she thought.

She paid little attention to Johann Thorburg's welcoming speech and to the notices that followed. She was glad when it was time to disperse to the studios for the morning ballet class. As her fingers touched the *barre* and she began to warm up she gained a little comfort. For one thing was certain: she had to work hard, so that her dreams of the future might one day be realized.

Chapter Six
At the Rehearsal Rooms

Anne certainly did work during the ballet class and was one of the few who did not get pulled up for some fault or for obvious lack of practising during the holidays. Anne always practised, for there was no difficulty about it at all. The studio at home was provided with a record player and many suitable records and she knew that she was lucky. Many others, living in small flats or over-crowded houses, found it almost impossible to keep up their ballet.

But when she went up to her classroom the feeling of depression returned. Lisa's empty place mocked her and it was little comfort when Fernanda – a nice girl, whose real home was in Spain – said tentatively:

"Would you like me to sit with you, Anne?"

Anne, conscious of ungraciousness in the cloakroom, tried to smile.

"Thank you, Fernanda. Yes, do. It's beastly without Lisa."

"She will be missing us, too."

"I don't really think so. It was her own choice, after all."

In break they all talked about holidays and afterwards there was an English lesson and some oral French.

Many in Anne's class stayed for lunch in the canteen,

and on that snowy morning even more than usual remained at school, because travelling was so difficult. In the warm, rather steamy atmosphere, sitting between Helenka and Colin, Anne did her best to be cheerful, but she knew that she was not her usual self. Still, it *was* nice to be back at the Thorburg amongst all the gossip about the Seniors, the members of the Company and the School staff, and she relaxed over her coffee.

Into the peaceful interlude came Carrie Gray, a contemporary of Delphine's. The Juniors never lingered in the canteen, but usually wandered away to their classroom or out into the square in good weather.

Carrie, a grave, rather plain child, tugged at Anne's sleeve.

"Please, Anne –!"

Anne looked up, startled and rather cross. It was not the first time that Carrie had sought her out after lunch and it usually meant that the wretched Delphine was in some trouble.

"What is it, Carrie?"

"I – I'm awfully sorry, but could you come? We – we're in trouble."

"Delphine?" Anne asked resignedly.

"Well, yes, in a way. But it's us who will get into the real trouble if someone doesn't help. Oh, *please* come!"

Colin and Helenka rose with Anne, both looking amused and curious, and the trio followed Carrie up the stairs and along corridors, Carrie explaining breathlessly over her shoulder as they went.

"You see, Delph was being impossible and we got sick of it. She does show off so frightfully, you know, Anne. And we – we put her in the record cupboard, meaning just for a few minutes. And – and we can't get the door undone. It's a miracle no one's heard her. She's making an awful row."

"Most of the Seniors are still in the canteen and I

suppose the staff are still in the staff room," said Colin, as they approached a small, nervous-looking group of Juniors, both boys and girls. Delphine, in the cupboard, was certainly making quite a noise, but the door was thick and her cries and thumps were muffled.

"She hasn't suffocated yet," said Carrie, with a sigh of relief.

"It would take more than that to suffocate *her*," said Anne and put her mouth near the crack. "Shut up, Delph! We'll get you out. There's no need to yell the school down."

"The key's in the lock," said Helenka and tried to turn it.

"Yes, Helenka," said a child called Gwen, who was in the class above Delphine. "But it's stuck or something. It just won't move."

"Let me out! I hate you all!" Delphine howled.

"We *honestly* didn't mean to –"

"Oh, she probably asked for it," said Anne.

The key had certainly stuck, refusing to turn at all. Colin wrenched it out, examined it, wiped off some rust and then tried again with no better result. Like most boys he had a penknife in his pocket and he scraped carefully inside the keyhole, while the Juniors looked nervously to right and left.

"On the first day of term!" Carrie groaned. "There'll be such a row if anyone catches us. They'll say we were bullying Delph."

Colin, still scraping industriously, muttered: "Rotten old door and rotten old key. There! I think that'll do it." And the key did turn. The door opened to reveal a scarlet-faced, furious Delphine, who burst out like an avenging angel, her curls on end.

"I might have *died* in there and it would have served you all right if you'd been *hung*!"

"Hanged," said Colin automatically. "They didn't mean it, you silly kid. It was an accident."

"It wasn't an accident that they shut me in there. And I was only saying that I was better than Gwen and she had no real right to the Big Doll's part in the Christmas Show."

"Then I don't wonder they shut you in. Pipe down, can't you?" Anne said angrily.

"We do get a little cross with her occasionally," said Carrie apologetically. "Oh, come on, Delph. We're sorry. But you do show off so frightfully."

"Yes, run along to your classrooms. The bell's just going," ordered Anne and watched the young ones obey. "Really it's a wonder Delph isn't the most unpopular girl in the school. But somehow she isn't. She can turn on the charm like a tap and they like her again." She sighed heavily. "But if *that's* how she's starting the term I hate to think how she'll end it. Thanks, Colin."

"Always ready to oblige," said Colin, grinning.

"And there's the bell! We'd better scoot." Anne led the way towards their classroom, thinking angry and uneasy thoughts about her troublesome young sister. Sometimes it seemed that nothing would make Delphine realize her humble part in the Thorburg scheme of things.

The rest of the week passed peacefully enough, though Anne was still in a depressed mood. Part of the trouble was that the weather was really too bad for her to go out at night, and, as soon as she had finished her homework, she was restless and, for almost the first time in her life, bored. She missed Lisa, finding their telephone conversations uneasy and thoroughly unsatisfactory.

The Thorburg School was by no means as warm as the house in Moone Crescent, for it was an old building in the main, though with newer studios and a hall built on behind. More than once the heating went wrong and they huddled into their cloaks even in the classrooms. One morning there was no water at all in the cloakrooms, there was ice on all the windows, and a number of the pupils were suffering from painful chilblains.

"It's past a joke," said Anne on Thursday afternoon, after she had walked nearly all the way home from Russell Square, with a protesting Delphine in tow. It was going to and from school that she missed Lisa most, she sometimes thought, and Delphine hated their mother's rule that she must travel with Anne. "How long is it going on for? At first I kind of liked it, and it's all right when you can see everywhere looking pretty in the snow – in the park, for instance – but I'm beginning to hate queueing and pushing and having a blue nose. And I'm filthy; we couldn't wash properly today."

Pelagia was just as articulate, for *she* had chilblains and the cold spell was something that she hardly knew how to endure.

"It's just awful! The rehearsal rooms are like the Arctic and it's not even as though I've got much to do. How *can* I look enchanted by all that's going on when I'm cold to the bone?"

"But you aren't only rehearsing *Casse Noisette*, are you?" Edward asked.

"No. We're also starting on the new Johann Thorburg ballet. It's just a short one, but nice and vigorous. It's the only time I'm ever *warm*!" wailed Pelagia, who had now taken to wearing three thick sweaters and sometimes Edward's smelly old sheepskin jacket as well. "I don't know how Mother still looks glamorous however cold it is. It's an art I haven't learned."

"I don't really feel the cold much," Mona Garland said mildly. "Though I must say it's pretty wicked waiting in the wings."

"Then there must be something wrong with my blood or

something. I wish I could go around wrapped in an electric blanket."

Joan, still cosily at home at Moone Crescent, listened with amused sympathy, and on Friday morning had a chance to see the present activites at the rehearsal rooms for herself. For her uncle said to her on Thursday evening, "Johann asked me if you'd call in and see him, Joan. He'll be at the rehearsal rooms about eleven tomorrow morning."

Joan looked and felt very much startled.

"Mr Thorburg wants to see *me*?"

"That's right. So will you go over there? You know where the rehearsal rooms are?"

Joan nodded, puzzled and rather uneasy. She had only met Johann Thorburg once, when she had been introduced to him after the students' Christmas Show and he had congratulated her on her ballet. *The Procession Passes*.

"You'll be able to watch some of the rehearsal," Pelagia remarked at breakfast. "We're going to concentrate on the Kingdom of Sweets this morning, so it means more blue fingers for me. I can't see why I have to be there, but the Company ballet mistress says that Little Clara should be present. Poor silly kid, grinning from her throne! We're putting it all together now. The party scene is really the most fun, though I can't bear John Lilling who's playing Franz. He's hateful in the ballet and not very nice in real life, but he's the youngest boy in the *corps*. Mother's coming this morning, so you'll see the Dance of the Sugar Plum Fairy."

Joan had never seen the ballet *Casse Noisette*, though she had read a beautifully illustrated book about it that Anne possessed and already had a mental picture of some of the scenes. So she felt both cheerful and curious as the bus carried her along the Euston Road. She left it by Euston Square and ran across the road to catch another bus by St Pancras Church.

"I'm a Londoner now!" she thought. "I know my way about and people often ask me the way."

The Thorburg Theatre was at the top of Kingsway, near the Tube station, but the rehearsal rooms were a little distance away in a narrow cutting off High Holborn. The wind was so keen that Joan almost ran the last part of the way, thinking that even a smelly sheepskin jacket would be welcome. There was certainly method in Pelagia's madness, for the cold went straight through her turquoise-blue coat and cardigan.

She gained the dark doorway with a fast beating heart and deep colour in her cheeks, and only then did nervousness engulf her. What on *earth* could the Director of the Thorburg School and Company want with humble Joan Bradshaw? Though he *had* said that one day they might put on her little ballet professionally. This, however, seemed wildly unlikely and Joan pushed the thought away.

She climbed the rather dreary stairs, hearing the sound of piano music in the distance. It was music that Joan knew from records, for Pelagia, who was immensely conscientious in spite of her moans about Little Clara, had played the ballet right through a number of times lately.

"*Danse Arabe*," thought Joan, advancing rather shyly. But no one took the least notice of her for some time. She stood near the door watching the *Danse Chinoise* and then the *Danse des Mirlitons*, and noting, with amused sympathy, that Pelagia was sitting on an upturned box at the side, still huddled, apparently, into all three sweaters, and with the sleeves of a fourth knotted round her neck.

Mona Garland was leaning against the piano, with her coat draped over her practice costume, and the *premier danseur*, William Royal, was beside her. Joan knew some of the other dancers by name and watched with increasing interest. The ignorant girl who had come to Moone Crescent had certainly not known an arabesque from a pirouette, but she had quickly learned the names of the different steps and movements from watching the endless practising in the studio at home. Since the success of her little ballet all the Garlands had been only too willing to explain.

"Because some knowledge of choreography can't hurt you," Anne had said on one occasion.

It was strange to see a ballet in the raw, and the everyday figures bore little relation to the cheerful characters who would later grace the Thorburg stage. The big, dreary room, the cold-looking woman at the piano, the dumpy, unimpressive appearance of the ballet mistress should have made it impossible to be able to visualize the not very distant opening night, yet when Mona Garland and William Royal came forward and began to dance Joan caught her breath. Later her aunt would be a real Sugar Plum Fairy. Now she was a slim woman of nearly forty in a black practice costume, and yet there was something about the assured, flashing dancing of the two principals that made Joan forget the cold, everything in the world but the sheer joy of a nearly perfect technique. This, as she well knew now, had been born of years and years of exercises at the *barre*, of classes and performances and then back to the basic exercises again, every day of the year.

It was some time – the *grand pas de deux* was almost over – before she realized that Johann Thorburg was standing at her side. At the end he touched her arm.

"Fine, wasn't it? They never give less than their best. Come with me, Joan." His voice still bore a trace of accent, for he had come from Switzerland as a young man.

Nervous again, Joan followed him into a small, rather dusty office, where an electric fire burned with comforting warmth. Johann Thorburg seated himself and motioned to Joan to take the other chair.

"We're not very grand here. I wish we could find some

new rehearsal rooms, but I suppose they suffice. We're not a rich company and accommodation costs so much in London. How are you these cold days? have you thought of any more ballets?"

Joan, blushing vividly, confessed that she hadn't.

"But I – I do mean to one day."

"I hope you will. That's why I asked you to come to see me. *The Procession Passes* was really most effective and I'm sure you could do others. Fairly short ballets are the thing we do best, being quite a small company. And we're always short of ideas."

Joan's colour drained away, leaving her very pale.

"But – but, Mr Thorburg, I'm still only a child really. You – you can't mean –"

"You're a clever girl with imaginative ideas. I'm not concerned with your age. Now, look! It's possible that some day we may lengthen *The Procession Passes* and take it into the repertoire, but it isn't quite what I'm looking for at the moment. I'm planning another continental tour, starting in May, and we shall probably do short ballets only. It's a tour of the smaller European theatres and I don't want to take *Coppélia* or *Casse Noisette*. I don't want to promise anything, but if you came up with any bright ideas … something in maybe two scenes that would run for about thirty minutes … well, just let me know. Or tell your uncle first and he'll pass it on to me."

Joan stumbled down the dark stairs, her thoughts whirling. She could hardly believe that the interview with Johann Thorburg had really happened. It was fantastic to think that he had asked *her* to plan something for the next continental tour. It could never happen, of course, that she would think of anything good enough, original enough, but it was wildly exciting and flattering all the same.

She didn't even notice the cold as she walked all the way back to Moone Crescent. And by the time she passed

Harley Street her fertile imagination was already working. Long ago, before she had ever dreamed that she would come to London, she had been taken by her Rochdale school to an exhibition of stage designs in Manchester, and this, coupled with two or three ballet performances she had seen on television, had given her embryonic ideas for a ballet of her own.

That, of course,, had been before she had any real conception of the true meaning and possibilities of ballet, and when at last she came to plan *The Procession Passes* those very first ideas had lain dormant. They had lain in her subconscious only to rear up now, as she walked blindly through London.

A ballet about that ill-fated Jacobite Rising of 1745, when the Highland army had marched on England. They had reached Manchester and then, furthest point south, Derby. But she remembered now that she had meant to concentrate on Manchester. Two scenes, one somewhere on the bleak hills and one in Manchester itself. There was a song called *Farewell, Manchester* and that – Joan came perilously near being run over as she crossed Baker Street – might be a good title.

A Scottish hero, a young man far from his own mountains, maybe falling in love during that halt of the Prince's army at Manchester. Or perhaps the girl was from the Lancashire moors and, when they fell in love, she followed the army south. They would be briefly happy, believing that the Prince would march in triumph to London and be crowned King. Of course this never happened; the army retreated from Derby and the whole romantic venture ended on Culloden Moor in the April rain and sleet. Maybe – Joan slipped on a patch of hard snow at this point – the lights lowered during the second scene, towards the end of it, while music showed what was happening, and then a messenger at last, telling the girl that her lover was dead.

The tune *Farewell, Manchester*, but mostly Scottish dance music and arrangements of Jacobite airs. *Charlie is My Darling … Will Ye No' Come Back Again*. Something sad to end with like *Lochaber No More*. No, it would have to end with *Farewell, Manchester* played again, fading gradually away.

Margaret knew nearly all the Scottish songs and dances and had records of many of them. So after lunch with Annali and Rosa in the kitchen – her uncle and aunt were lunching out – Joan set off for her friend's house in Sussex Mews. She was still half-lost in the bursting, growing ideas and pictures and she just *had* to hear the music.

Margaret was at home and she listened with interest to the morning's happenings; then she rose eagerly and began to sort the records. They lay on cushions on the floor by the electric fire, and Joan listened and accepted and rejected in her own mind, without saying much to Margaret. At this stage the ballet could not really be talked about and she knew that her friend understood.

She walked home in the dark at a quarter to five, humming a Highland march and wondering if Mr Thorburg could fit ballet steps to it. So much would depend on that. But the thing was growing and growing and she was lost in the triumph of creation.

It was quite a shock to find that Anne and Delphine had arrived and were in the living-room with Pelagia and their mother. Joan blinked at the family gathering, coming back only slowly from her own absorbing thoughts.

"No one ever listens to *me*!" Delphine was crying. "Oh, Mother, there's a new girl; a new Junior. She had a cold and couldn't come till today. Her name's Binnie Byrne and we're going to be best friends and –"

"I hope she's a sensible child, then," said her mother.

Delphine tossed up her beret and caught it just before Bonne-Bouche could grab it.

"Oh, sensible! Who wants a sensible friend? She's got nearly black hair, and Irish eyes – blue as anything, with thick dark lashes – and she didn't want to come to the Thorburg *at all.*"

Anne, who had heard about Binnie Byrne all the way home, chipped in, "I haven't seen the kid, Mother, but she's the daughter of someone who was once in the Thorburg *corps*. She never even got a solo part, and she was fed up and left to get married. Now she wants her Binnie to be a great ballerina, because *she* never managed it. According to Delph."

Mona Garland frowned and then said: "You must mean Belinda Anne Connor. I remember her quite well. *She* had black hair and Irish eyes and she left the Company in some dudgeon, saying that it was jealousy that kept her from being given solo roles. But in fact, though she was so pretty, she wasn't a very good dancer or very reliable. I did meet her once in a restaurant a few years ago, and she was with her husband, an Irishman called Byrne. He's something quite important in the City, I believe. How old is the girl?"

"She's ten. Three days older than me."

"Well, why didn't she want to go to the Thorburg?"

"Because she really wants to go to a stage school, where she'd learn everything, not just ballet and character. She's had parts in two films – imagine how exciting! I wish I could. And she begged and begged, but her mother's quite set on her being a ballerina."

"Good heavens!" said Mona Garland faintly. "I hope she isn't disappointed, then."

"You know, I've often thought *I'd* do better at a stage school," her youngest child remarked, on her way out of the room. "They set more store on *personality*. What's the matter, Joan? You look moonstruck!"

"Nothing," said Joan brusquely.

She followed Delphine up the stairs, and Anne and her mother, left alone with Pelagia, looked at each other ruefully.

"Someone like Carrie Gray would be far better for Delph," Anne said. "She just *would* make friends with another rebel!"

"I must ask Johann about that Binnie child," Mona Garland remarked. "But we can't really try and choose Delphine's friends for her. She has, as she's always saying, personality, and she's also extremely obstinate. She'll go her own way until something pulls her up really sharply. And I only hope she doesn't get hurt in the process."

Chapter Seven
Edward's Girlfriend

The Garlands always did their weekend homework on Friday evenings, in order to get it out of the way, but Joan was still free and she spent most of the evening alone at the top of the house, playing the studio piano. When she wasn't playing she simply sat staring into space, trying to visualize her ballet as a whole. And by the time she went to bed she was in a panic, sure that never again would the miracle occur. She was convinced that *The Procession Passes* had been a strange kind of inspiration and one that could never be repeated.

But in the middle of the night she awoke seeing things quite differently. She lay in the warm darkness, listening to the howling of the wind, her mind working feverishly. She had been thinking on the wrong lines, that was clear to her now. She had been thinking too sentimentally. *Farewell, Manchester* would be sad in essence, a tragedy, but it would have to be treated in a very modern manner. True, it was history, or based on history, but it would have to be done in something like the way the Royal Ballet had treated the Greek legends, *Antigone* and *Electra*.

The two backcloths must be stark, simple impressions of the Lancashire moors and perhaps a Manchester square, and the Highland costumes must be suggested rather than copied exactly. As for the music, it might be all right to use Jacobite airs and Highland marches, but they would have to be quickened, perhaps altered, and welded into an interesting and balletic score.

Joan thanked heaven that her uncle was an able composer and had already done the music for two or three Thorburg ballets, as well as arranging the Northern and Russian airs for *The Procession Passes*. He would understand what she wanted, when she knew definitely herself. She imagined a lot of drums and woodwinds, and maybe violins suggesting the bagpipes, as Arnold had done in *Tam O'Shanter*.

"I need to know a lot of things," Joan thought, growing sleepy again at last, and, as soon as she could the next day, she slipped off to the nearest reference library in a search for books that would show her Highland and English dress of the eighteenth century and for old prints of Manchester at the same period. In the afternoon she made her way to the National Portrait Gallery, where she believed there were several Jacobite pictures, including a famous one of Prince Charles Edward Stuart.

"Joan's being mysterious," said Delphine, during high tea. Pelagia and her mother were dancing that evening, and Edwin Garland was conducting, though all had been free in the afternoon.

Anne, who had been to a film with Lisa, had come in late and was rather silent, as she so often was these days. It was Lisa who had suggested the film and she had gone gladly, but during tea afterwards the familiar tension had built up between them. Lisa had asked about the week at the Thorburg and Anne had told her as vividly as she could, but it seemed so extraordinary to be describing events at the ballet school to Lisa that she had grown more and more stiffly miserable.

Sitting on the arm of the chair and watching the others eat, she said, "What do you mean, Delph? Why is Joan mysterious?"

Delphine flicked her bright glance over her cousin's slightly reddened cheeks.

"Well, she just *is*. She's got a – a preoccupied air, and she went to the National Portrait Gallery and wouldn't say why. And last night, when we were all doing our homework, she was playing like a mad thing in the studio."

"How did you hear if you were supposed to be working?" Joan demanded.

"Because I went up to my room for a book. Do tell, Joan! Is it another ballet?"

"Don't tease her," Mona Garland said, a little sharply. Delphine's chatter always disturbed her before a performance.

"I'm *not* teasing her. I'm just interested. I knew one of those tunes, Joan. Well, of course I know *Charlie is My Darling*, but I know *Farewell, Manchester*. We sang it in school last term. It's a mouldy thing; it has silly words."

"The words don't concern me," said Joan. "Or only in that they partly gave me the idea. Look here! I *don't* want to talk about it."

Edwin Garland glanced at his niece with amused respect. Johann Thorburg had told him what he had said to Joan, so there probably was another ballet on the way, but he knew full well that they wouldn't hear much until the girl was ready. Creative thought could not be hurried, and it could usually not be talked about. To talk about growing ideas often weakened them, he believed.

Pelagia, for once tactful, broke in with a remark about Timothy, who was inconsolable because he had seen so little of her lately, and the rest of the meal passed without further reference to Joan's mysterious behaviour.

On Sunday afternoon, which was bright, but as bitterly cold as always, Anne went up to Hampstead Heath with Colin Corbett, another boy called Bill Wright, and Fernanda. They took their skates with them, since the boys had said they were fed up with playing safe and it was more than time that they all enjoyed the ice. Fernanda could hardly skate at all and had to be instructed and held, and they spent a merry two hours until dusk fell over the vast, snowy landscape.

"Why didn't we ask Lisa?" Colin enquired, as they made their way to the bus stop, on their way home.

"I did," Anne said, "but they were having some family friends to tea."

She had enjoyed the afternoon, but the mention of Lisa brought back in full force her mood of sadness and depression, and she got ready for school the next morning with a strong "Monday morning" feeling. Nothing went right. A button came off her blouse ... then she found that a necessary book was not in her case.

"Oh, you go on!" she said impatiently to Delphine, as she dashed back upstairs. The book was under her bed – how on *earth* had it got there? – and she thundered down again, grabbing up her case and gloves, and shouted to anyone who was listening: " 'Bye!"

Only Joan, coming down the stairs behind her in her red Scott-Smithson uniform, answered her, and Anne flung herself out of doors, nearly falling head first down the steps.

"I hate Mondays!" she muttered to herself, as the icy wind caught her and sent the ends of her scarf into one eye. The eye immediately began to water and she blinked fiercely as she hurried to the end of the crescent. And there, as in the old days, was Lisa. Only now she wore the Scott-Smithson uniform and carried a leather satchel over her shoulder.

Anne stared at her and Lisa stared back, then smiled.

"Hullo, Anne! Delph said you hadn't gone. You're late today."

"Lost a beastly book and breakfast was late because of the power cut," Anne said gruffly. "I – I forgot I might see you."

"I'm waiting for Joan. She said we'd better be early, as it's the first day of term. Oh, there's Margaret!" And Lisa waved.

"Joan's just on the way," said Anne. "And I must fly or I'll *never* get there in time." She added belatedly, over her shoulder: "Good luck, Lisa: I – I hope you enjoy it."

She looked back once more and saw Lisa hurrying towards Margaret MacAllister and Joan just coming down the steps and after that the morning seemed bleaker than ever.

"I shall never get used to it," she thought wretchedly.

Lisa, walking briskly towards Dorset Square between Joan and Margaret, was not without her own share of sadness. She knew that Anne had not forgiven her for giving up dancing, or perhaps it would be more true to say that Anne had not yet come to terms with the idea. Their recent meetings, as Lisa well knew, had not been a success, but she seemed powerless to do anything about it. She was most genuinely looking forward to her new life – though a little nervous on that first morning – and it would be impossible to pretend otherwise just to help Anne. Lisa had had her very bad time, but her father had been so kind and understanding about her wishes that she had believed all would be well. She had certainly believed that she and Anne would remain friends, perhaps with even more than usual to talk about because of their separate experiences, but it looked as though it was not to be.

Lisa was not shy – she had mixed with boys and girls for years at the Thorburg – and she saw no reason why, in a few days, she should not be quite at home at the

Scott-Smithson School. So she followed Joan and Margaret quite confidently, saw her name ticked off a list and was presently taken to the hall for the First Assembly by her two faithful companions. They both gave her a good deal of whispered information as the school waited for Miss Smithson to appear on the platform, and the only things that seemed really strange to Lisa were that there were no boys and that no ballet class would follow.

Ballet ... well, there would be no ballet classes ever again and Lisa was not sorry; it was just that habit made her feel that a ballet class must inevitably follow morning assembly. They went up to a large classroom overlooking the pleasant symmetry of Dorset Square, with the snow-covered gardens in the middle, and Lisa was given books and a timetable.

She was an ordinary girl at last at an ordinary school and the knowledge gave her definite satisfaction. It was almost as though a burden had rolled off her to know that now she could give her full attention to other things. To languages, in particular, for it had been arranged that Lisa was to have extra French and Spanish. German she already spoke and read fluently, and later she thought that she might learn Russian.

Margaret and Joan sat together, but Lisa shared the next desk with a girl called Selina Blane. Lisa liked and admired Joan and found the pretty, delicate-looking Peggy – she had never realized the Gaelic spelling of the name was Peigi – most attractive. She had such a lovely speaking voice, like Welsh, but softer. And she was friendly and kind.

Altogether, thought Lisa, settling down to the first class of the day, an English literature lesson, the Scott-Smithson looked as though it would be fine. But through her mind, at that moment, flitted a picture of Anne's face when they met in the crescent.

"She'll get used to it one day," Lisa told herself, opening *Julius Caesar*. "She'll have to. And then everything will be just right again."

It was during that same day that Edward overheard a disturbing conversation. He had lost his handkerchief somehow during morning school, and, remembering that he had another in his coat pocket, went down to the cloakroom to get it. Three cloakrooms were reserved for the boys at the end of the basement passage and the partitions did not quite go up to the top. And suddenly a voice said from the other side of the partition:

"Girls! Don't talk to me about girls! One stood me up last night. I waited for an hour in the cold."

"I make it a rule never to wait for more than twenty minutes," said another voice, belonging to a boy in an upper class whom Edward knew quite well and liked. "By the way, did you know that Garland's been dating Tarn Marlow? You were rather struck on her at one time, weren't you?"

"Briefly. I soon saw through her. You mean you've seen them together?"

"Yes, a couple of times, and I was quite surprised, because old Ed's never seemed to show the slightest interest in girls. Got enough of them around him at home, probably, though the Garland girls are an attractive lot. My cousin goes to the Scott-Smithson and bears out what you say – what you imply, rather. She says Tarn's a nasty bit of work, and she's not the jealous kind. A jolly sensible girl, my cousin."

"Garland's old for his age and all that. He probably knows what she's like."

"Well, I rather hope so, because she's saying blatantly that she wants to meet Mona Garland; that that's why she's putting up with Garland. Rotten thing to say, when he's such a nice chap. But she seems to be nothing but a cheap little celebrity hunter."

Edward found his handkerchief and walked away towards the canteen. The words of the two older boys still rang through his head. His first reaction was that they were jealous. The boy who had been "rather struck on" Tarn probably wished that *he* were going out with her, sitting beside her in the cinema and the theatre. Tarn was so lovely, and Edward, not usually blind, had not tried to look beyond her attractive face and beguiling ways.

Tarn was the first girl who had ever appealed to him in just that way and he had never doubted that she liked him, too, and took pleasure in their meetings. Edward was not particularly conceited, but he knew that he was quite good-looking and hoped that he was intelligent.

He tried hard to forget the words he had overheard, yet by the end of afternoon school he had remembered how often Tarn had suggested that he take her to his home, the questions she had asked about his father and mother, her evident desire to be taken to the Thorburg Theatre. And he, not wanting to face his curious and probably critical family – but why had he thought they would be critical of Tarn? – had evaded the issue all along the line. He had also remembered the way that Tarn sprinkled her conversation with references to the important people that she or her family knew, and the poison was well and truly in his soul.

But he still wanted to see Tarn and was looking forward to their next meeting. Life had been so much more exciting just lately, and he couldn't, wouldn't, believe that Tarn was only interested in him because he happened to have a famous mother. He convinced himself several times that there was nothing in the words he had overheard, but they were not to be forgotten, all the same. Edward was both shaken and unhappy, and he knew that he would not feel right until he had seen Tarn again. He told himself that it was natural that she should be interested in his family; in Edward's experience most people were, but that was all there was to it. And one day, but certainly not yet, he *would* take Tarn home.

During the next few days Joan tried to comfort Anne by telling her how happy Lisa seemed at the Scott-Smithson. For, to Joan's mind, if you had a friend you wanted her to be happy, and it had not yet occurred to her that a large part of Anne's trouble was jealousy. So Anne listened to all the well-meant remarks about Lisa's first days at the new school, and, though she *was* glad that Lisa was settling down, she also suffered a good deal because her friend seemed daily to go further away from her.

Lisa on the telephone did nothing to alter this idea, now it was so firmly fixed in Anne's mind. Lisa, in her turn, talked of Joan, saying many times how kind and friendly Joan and Margaret were being.

So Anne went on being quietly, drearily miserable, and this feeling was not helped by the continuing bitter weather. There were days when the buses and trains were badly affected and when Anne and Delphine had to walk all the way home, arriving tired and cold. Not that Delphine really minded snow and frost, though she continued to grumble because she had to return home with Anne, and if she could have escaped her sister's after-school vigilance she would have done. But Anne was conscientious about this, though secretly so unwilling, and on the one occasion when she saw Delphine trying to slip away with Binnie gave her such a lecture, and vowed such dire consequences if it happened again while it was so cold and dark and travelling was so difficult, that Delphine shrugged and obeyed.

Delphine was enjoying her second week back at the Thorburg, though it was doubtful if her form mistress was enjoying her presence. During the ballet classes Delphine worked, because pride would not let her do anything else – pride and perhaps family habit – but these feelings did not extend to her school work, which she generally did in a sketchy, haphazard way. Her elders made her concentrate on her homework, much to Delphine's fury, but in class she lacked concentration and giggled so much with her new friend Binnie Byrne that they were presently put to sit at opposite ends of the classroom.

By the time Binnie had been in the school for a week she was even more of a by-word than Delphine, for she was a natural rebel and also had much Irish blood. On the whole her attitude was the casual Irish one of "What harm?", and she said often that if the Thorburg didn't like her then she would get her wish and go to a stage school and maybe make another film, which the Thorburg wouldn't allow. The Thorburg *did* like her dancing, for she had excellent technique for so young a child, but not only the form mistress, Miss Grant, but others in authority had early marked her down as a possible source of trouble.

"What were you *doing* after lunch?" Anne asked indignantly, when, having had to wait for Delphine after school, her sister arrived with a rush. "Why did you have to stay behind now?"

"Oh, only to be lectured," Delphine said airily. "Binnie and I weren't doing anything really. If two of the Seniors hadn't come along and taken us to Miss Grant no one would have known a thing about it, or not until we had the next record concert, and now it's all spoilt. We'd only just *started* mixing up the records –"

Anne sighed, seizing her sister's arm and hauling her out into Russell Square.

"Anyone would think you were *five*. What an absolutely idiotic thing to do! And now we're late and *look* at the queues! We'd better try for a train. I don't feel like walking, and if we don't get our homework done before dinner we'll have it hanging over us all weekend. It was silly of Miss Grant to make you so late."

"There wasn't time to deal with us before afternoon school. She said she was sorry when I got in a word and explained you were waiting," Delphine said, with a good deal of injured innocence.

It was already dark, but there seemed to be something wrong with the street lighting. The lights in the Thorburg had been dim, too, just before they left. Anne, striding gloomily towards the nearest tube station, said, "I believe there's another power cut. Yes, *look* at the people here! The trains are stuck or something. Oh, well, it will have to be a bus, if we can get on one."

The power cut was still on when they reached home; the house was lighted by candles and the central heating was down almost to nothing. Annali was grumbling that the dinner would be ruined and Edward had such an air of gloomy despair that Anne could not fail to notice it.

"What's the matter with *you*?"

"Oh, nothing."

"Well, it must be something."

"If you must know I'm supposed to be taking Tarn to that special showing of the Russian ballet film. Mother got tickets for me; they're very hard to get."

"Well, they're showing it again. I'm going later."

"But I want to go *tonight*, and if this blessed power cut goes on –" And Edward, feeling he had said more than enough, walked upstairs to his room.

Pelagia, with a warm rug over her, was lying on the sofa, eating chocolates as a preliminary to the high tea that she and her father were to have alone that evening. That day had seen the first dress rehearsal of *Casse Noisette*, and there was to be another on Monday, with the first night on Tuesday.

"How did it go?" Anne asked, sinking down exhaustedly.

"Oh, not so bad. It's always miraculous how things come together. Mr Thorburg said I was a very *fetching* Little

Clara," Pelagia said languidly. "And the theatre was quite warm. But if this weather goes on much longer I shall make myself a nice little woolly suit, trousers and top all in one, and zip myself into it for the rest of the winter."

"And wear it under your nightgown during *Casse Noisette?*" asked Delphine, helping herself to a chocolate.

"There might be sense in it at that," said her sister. "The nightgown is so thin you can practically see through it."

"To naked you?"

"Not naked; I have tights on, as you know perfectly well."

The early ones, joined by Edward, sat down to half-warmed soup and cold meat, but the power came on fully in time for Annali to have hopes of saving the dinner. Edward, looking unusually spick and span, and much more cheerful, departed in a rush and his family smiled indulgently.

"He *has* got it badly!" said Delphine.

Edward scarcely noticed the bitter cold of the evening as he walked briskly towards George Street. All week he had been thinking about Tarn, sometimes believing the words he had overheard, sometimes not, and now that he was actually going to see her again he definitely did not believe them at all.

Tarn greeted him charmingly, and, as they went by bus to the small cinema where the film was being shown, Edward was very happy. He thought the film excellent and was enjoying every minute of it, but about half-way through he became aware that Tarn was restless. She yawned a number of times and presently muttered that she was cold. The cinema certainly wasn't very warm, but Edward took her hand and tried to convince himself that everything was all right.

But Tarn, kept on yawning, and occasionally sighing gustily, and he began to admit to himself, with dismay, that he had been wrong in thinking the film would interest her. He ought to have known quite well that Tarn knew little about ballet and would have preferred something light-hearted, a comedy or an American musical.

He was hardly prepared, however, for the savage little voice in which she said, as they were leaving the cinema, "*Well*! I've rarely been so bored or so cold. What on earth made you take me to that, Edward?"

Before Edward could answer they both saw that it was snowing, and Tarn shivered exaggeratedly.

"*Oh*! Isn't this the *end*? It will just have to be a taxi. If you can get one." Her tone clearly implied that Edward was mostly unlikely to accomplish this feat, and Edward himself had doubts, since many other people seemed to have the same idea. But if Tarn wanted to go home by taxi, even if it took his last effort and most of his remaining pocket-money, then a taxi must be found.

Eventually he was successful and handed Tarn into the the slight warmth. She sank back and he could just see her petulant face.

"Look, Tarn, I'm sorry. I really thought you'd like the film. We'll go to something *you* choose next time."

"Next time!" said Tarn. "Why can't you ask me to dinner at your home? I thought that knowing you would be so interesting. I thought that you had all sorts of wonderful parties, and entertained famous people."

Edward, by then, was not only chilled to the bone, with very wet feet, but quite violently unhappy. He felt – in spite of the warning earlier in the week – as though he had a stranger beside him, a stranger with a sharp voice and features that looked curiously sharper, too, in the dim light. But he had plenty of pride, and pride won. He said in a steady, cool voice:

"We *do* have parties very occasionally, and it's true that famous people do come to our house. But we're a very ordinary, hard-working family, Tarn. There are many evenings when Father, Mother and Pelagia are all at the theatre. Of course I should be glad to take you home sometime, but you wouldn't find it very exciting."

At which Tarn made a little sound that was certainly not pretty and said, "Well, *you're* not very exciting, either. That awful film!"

And after that they didn't speak at all until the taxi skidded to a stop outside Tarn's home. Edward stepped out into the whirling flakes and Tarn swept past him, without saying good-night. He waited until she had disappeared indoors and then told the taxi driver to go to Moone Crescent.

When he reached home he went straight up to his room, knowing that some members of his family were in the living-room, but not caring if they thought his behaviour strange.

In the morning he emerged looking grave and remote and it was months before anyone heard anything at all about that disastrous evening. Edward never saw Tarn again, except in the distance, but it was quite a long time before he ceased to miss her prettiness and the nameless magic she had had for him; a long time, too, before he managed to get the dreadful memory of her sharp voice and altered face out of his mind.

Chapter Eight
Casse Noisette

Joan spent the cold weekend mostly in the solitude of the studio or her own room, working on her ballet. She had not dared to dwell on it too much during the week, but all the same her ideas and her knowledge had been imperceptibly growing. She had found that Margaret was a good source of information about the Rising of 1745, for it was a period that had always fascinated her. Margaret also possessed a book of Scottish tartans, which Joan had borrowed.

Now, with forty-eight hours in which she could really get to work, she was lost, far from the real world. It was the same true pleasure in creation that had filled her when *The Procession Passes* had begun to grow. On Saturday she painted feverishly almost all day, creating and rejecting and creating again, until she had the two backcloths roughed out, and also many of the costume designs done in rough. The backcloth for the first scene was stark and telling, showing the bare, rounded shapes of the moors, here and there pale gold with the great sweeps of the moor grass, and a wintry sky behind. For the Jacobite Army had marched through Lancashire in November on their way to Derby and that fatal – but then unimagined – decision to turn back and not risk London.

In the left foreground was an impression of one of the farmhouses that Joan knew so well, and at first she made it nearly black, then realized that in the middle of the eighteenth century the stone would still be its natural grey-gold. For no smoke had polluted the northern air at that time.

The second backcloth was based on an old print of Manchester that she had found in a book borrowed from the library.

Another book had given her some idea of the type of simple clothes northern farming folk might have worn, and these she laboured to simplify even more, so that they would be suitable for dancing. For Joan now understood the necessity to make sure that clothes would be comfortable during violent movement.

Colour there would be in plenty from the Highland costumes, but she decided to keep the tartans down to as few as possible: Royal Stuart for the Prince, and, for the rest of the army, MacDonald of Clanranald, Cameron of Lochiel and, at most, two others. Margaret's book of tartans also included some pictures of how the Highland dress was worn at that time, not so very long before it ceased, by English law, to be worn in Scotland. Joan's first attempts were too close, she realized, to reality, but after hours of work she designed something that was authentic enough, while being a more suitable costume for ballet.

She had been learning all the time she had been living with the Garlands, but there were still great gaps in her knowledge, so many ballets she had never seen. At five o'clock on the Saturday she heard Anne on the floor below and leaned over the banister to call to her.

Anne looked up into her cousin's flushed face and noted the untidy hair and the streak of red paint on her cheek.

"What's going on? Is it really a new ballet? You might tell!"

"I will tell when it's done. I'm still in the throes. Anne, I want to know something. You've seen *Solitaire*, haven't you? I remember hearing you talk about it. Isn't that the ballet that starts with something hanging down from the flies? A banner? A motif?"

Anne put one foot on the bottom stair.

"Yes, it's a kind of great orange motif, a bit tattered and with a queer face on it. Pel has it on the sleeve of her Arnold record if you want to see it. He did the music, you know. Why are you interested?"

"It's not a banner?"

"Well, not really. I don't think it means anything. If it does it was too obscure for *me*. It disappears pretty soon."

"Thanks; that's all I wanted to know. Would it matter if I copied the idea with a real banner?"

"I shouldn't think so. Look here –"

But Joan had gone to look at a picture she had found of the Royal Standard of Scotland, gold with a red lion.

On Sunday, with the designs done in rough to her satisfaction, Joan turned to music and played until she was worn out, again accepting and rejecting and occasionally jumping up to try and dance, while humming the tune.

"Oh, heavens!" she said aloud, at one point. "If I were a ballet dancer it would be a lot easier." But she would not appeal to anyone in the house at such an early stage, though there were times when it would have helped to ask Edward's assistance. She would have liked to see what movements he would have put spontaneously to the marches in particular.

At dusk she went over to Margaret's to hear some of the Scottish records again, and when she returned just in time for dinner, tired and bemused, she found the family declaring that they had heard quite enough of the music for *Casse Noisette*.

"Pel's played it all afternoon down here," Anne groaned. "She's getting all worked up about Tuesday."

Pelagia did, in fact, look unusually pale and nervy, and was announcing loudly that if she felt like this about being Little Clara in a beastly nightgown heaven only knew how she would survive more exacting roles.

"She'll be all right on the night," Mona Garland said to Joan, when they were alone together for a moment.

It was then that Joan asked a question that had been in her mind for some time.

"But if she doesn't like that role is she going to be good enough? Won't people realize how she feels?"

Her aunt laughed.

"Oh, don't worry. She does like it. She's thrilled to the marrow to be in the limelight. Of course she's soon going to be capable of something far more lyrical or dramatic, but you don't know Pel yet if you can't see through her façade."

"But – but she's moaned for weeks, all about what Timothy will think, and about the nightgown and all the rest. And she's always cold, she says."

"She doesn't, I'm afraid, really care at all about what poor Timothy thinks, and in any case he'd adore her if she was one of the Ugly Sisters. She *will* be cold during the Kingdom of Sweets act. No one can say it's warm backstage during this terrible weather and she'll have to sit in the draughts and look as though she's happy. But Pel will be all right. Everyone will love her."

Joan decided that there certainly were things she still had to learn about ballet and the Garland family if Pelagia's behaviour of the last few weeks was going to lead to a perfect performance.

On Tuesday morning Pelagia had her photograph in the *Daily Mail*, a head and shoulders portrait as Little Clara, with her loose and shining hair tied back with a ribbon, Alice fashion, and the round neck of the famous nightgown making her look just a child.

"Miss Pelagia Garland, one of the youngest members of

the Thorburg Company, is dancing the role of Little Clara in tonight's new production of the ballet *Casse Noisette* at the Thorburg Theatre," said the accompanying paragraph. And went on to point out that Pelagia was, of course, the daughter of the famous ballerina, Mona Garland.

It seemed very strange to Joan that the subject of the news paragraph was sitting opposite to her, tucking away her usual substantial breakfast.

Joan was looking forward very much to the evening, when she, Anne, Delphine, Lisa and Margaret MacAllister were all going to the first night. Timothy was going, too, but had made sure of his usual seat in the stalls. The Garlands, from choice, generally sat in the front row of the Circle on special occasions, greatly preferring that position to one of the stage boxes. Delphine was the only one who would have preferred a box, because she enjoyed being conspicuous.

Edward, asked to join the girls' party, had said a trifle curtly that he was going with Jocheli Thorburg.

Joan, first home from school as usual, stood in the hall and listened in puzzlement to what seemed to be a low intoning from the living-room. It was far more usual to come in to orchestral music, played very loudly.

She opened the door cautiously and found Pelagia in her usual prone position on the sofa, but, instead of a box of chocolates, she now had a large volume propped up on her chest. Joan at once recognized it as the Oxford Dictionary of Quotations.

" 'Come away, come away, death,
And in sad cypress let me be laid;
Fly away, fly away, breath –'

Oh, hullo, Joan!"

"What on earth are you doing?" Joan demanded, dropping her satchel and staring at the pale face of her eldest cousin.

"Well, I felt so awful that I remembered something Mother says. She was always terribly nervous when she was dancing new roles when she was young and she used to say poetry aloud to calm herself. I tried just saying it from memory and I couldn't get beyond one line. You know – 'Friends, Romans,, countrymen, lend me your ears ...' and perfect blank. So I got up and fetched this." Pelagia flipped back through the pages. "Listen, Joan. I've read bits of Swinburne and even Tennyson, but Shakespeare is the best to real aloud." And Pelagia read:

" 'Fear no more the heat o' the sun,
Nor the furious winter's rages;
Thou thy wordly task hast done,
Home art gone and ta'en thy wages;
Golden lads and girls all must,
As chimney-sweepers, come to dust.' "

Her voice was beautiful, warm and clear, and, as she read on through the verses, Joan stood very still, caught up in the beauty of the words and in some quality of the lovely, indolent girl before her. "Golden lads and girls all must ..." Pelagia was young, with most of her life before her. It seemed impossible to think of her as ever being old, coming to dust, but Joan was suddenly conscious of the transience of life, filled with the knowledge that everything would pass. Misery and happiness and the wild, rapturous certainty of being alive would all, some day, come to an end.

Pelagia flipped again, almost to the beginning of the book.

" 'This ae nighte, this ae nighte,
– *Every nighte and alle*, –
Fire and fleet and candle-lighte,
And Christe receive thy saule.' "

Pelagia then looked up and saw her cousin's face.

"*Joan*! What on earth is it? You're crying!"

"Not really." But Joan was blinking fiercely, much ashamed to be caught out in such a display of emotion. "It's just – you just – Why on earth aren't you an actress instead of a dancer?"

Pelagia, amused, dropped the heavy book on the floor with a thud.

"I've sometimes fancied it myself, let me tell you. I'd adore to be Ophelia. I'd make everyone's flesh creep in the mad scene."

"I've no doubt you would," Joan agreed drily and went slowly up to her room. "Fire and fleet and candle-lighte –"

"No wonder Timothy wants her," she thought, as she began to lay out her things for the evening. "In a way she's the most remarkable of them all. Delph will be something showy, maybe a film star or famous in musical comedy, but Pelagia *could* be great."

For once Pelagia ate almost nothing. She looked white and more ethereal than usual and was nervously anxious to be off. It was not snowing, but was an icy, brilliant evening, with the stars already out.

"I have to be early. I just have to be!" she kept on wailing, and in the end her father fetched the car and drove away with his wife and eldest daughter. Lisa was travelling with her father, but Margaret joined the others in Moone Crescent and they went grandly to the Thorburg in a taxi, muffled up in warm coats and scarves, but with their prettiest dresses underneath.

"Because people always look at the Garlands," said Delphine.

"You self-conscious little horror!" cried Anne, who was nervous on Pelagia's behalf. Anne and Lisa had not met for some time, but when they came together in the theatre there was little opportunity to talk about anything but the coming ballet. Then, as the minutes ticked away and the members of the orchestra began to tune up, they all fell rather silent.

Joan sank back between Lisa and Margaret, conscious that those ancient, fearsome words were still ringing through her head. "Fire and fleet and candle-lighte –" But Pelagia was going to be a child at a party, and then in the Land of Snow and the Kingdom of Sweets. She was not going to be ringed by the atmosphere of an old ballad.

Down here, behind the heavy curtain, the dancers would already be warming up. It was almost time … her uncle appeared, to considerable applause. The music began.

The curtain rose on the Prologue, showing the front door of the house and the guests arriving for the Christmas party. Then the painted drop-scene disappeared and there was the party, with Little Clara and her brother Fritz reaching up to the lighted Christmas tree. Little Clara! Pelagia, in an old-fashioned blue dress, with frilly pantaloons showing beneath her full skirts, and looking, indeed, not much more than ten years old.

The whole thing seemed so extraordinary that Joan missed some of the story. It was by no means the first time she had seen Pelagia dance, but she had always been one of the crowd. Now, though certainly at a crowded party, she was very much to the fore with her unpleasant brother Fritz. Presently Little Clara had a short solo dance and the audience applauded warmly, the mechanical toys were a great success and the scene moved on, with the breaking of the Nutcracker Doll, the departure of the guests, and the children being sent up to bed. For a short while the stage was empty, and dark except for the lights on the Christmas tree, and then Little Clara came creeping back, this time wearing her nightgown, to seek her broken Nutcracker Doll. And almost at once she was involved in the battle between the soldiers and the mice, rescuing the Nutcracker

Prince by banging the King of the Mice on the head with her slipper.

The scene changed magically to the Land of Snow, with Little Clara borne aloft by the glittering Prince. Little Clara certainly looked starry-eyed and enchanted by the wonderful thing that was happening to her.

The Snow Queen (Barbary Brown) and the snowflakes danced, drifting about gracefully in front of the frosty backcloth, and the curtain came down to applause that, if not wild, was extremely appreciative.

"Is that really Pelagia?" Margaret asked, as the house lights went up. "She looks younger than Anne. Almost younger than Delphine."

"One day *I* shall be Little Clara!" Delphine cried shrilly, and a voice said very audibly behind them, "Yes, the Garland children. The two redheads. charming, aren't they?"

Delphine turned round and gave them her best smile.

When the curtain rose again it was to show the vivid set for the Kingdom of Sweets, and the Prince led Little Clara on stage, introducing her to the Sugar Plum Fairy. Then Little Clara was sitting on her throne at the side of the stage, ready to watch the entertainment that had been arranged for her. If she was in a draught she was certainly managing to keep up a delightful appearance of eagerness and pleasure as the various dancers appeared. The *Danse Espagnole*, the *Danse Arabe*, the *Danse Chinoise*, and so on until the Waltz of the Flowers and the big moment of the ballet, the *Grand Pas de Deux*.

And once again Joan was filled with amazement, for it was strange to think that the Sugar Plum Fairy dancing so flashingly on the Thorburg stage was her own aunt, whom she had last heard admonishing Delphine for borrowing her best lipstick.

"Go and wash it off, for heaven's sake!" she had said,

almost at the moment of stepping into the car, and now she was a fairylike figure, far removed from everyday affairs.

Little Clara kept up the delighted appearance of interest to the very end, looking so charming and childish that the strange little episode of the afternoon at last faded from Joan's mind.

Down near the front of the stalls Timothy Blandford stared at his girl and thought, "Good Heavens! Have I been baby-snatching?" He felt very peculiar indeed when he remembered how often he had asked Pelagia to marry him, and how often he had visualized her as a bride.

The end of the ballet was very near. Little Clara leaped up and mingled with the dancers. The curtain came swishing down and then rose again and again. Mona Garland and William Royal took several curtains, then Mona Garland alone, when she was presented with several bouquets. Finally the two principals appeared in front of the curtain, each holding a hand of Little Clara. Pelagia curtseyed and smiled, tossing back her hair.

"Good old Pel!" Anne murmured. "She was one of the nicest Little Claras I've ever seen. But I bet she's glad that's over."

The evening ended with one of the new Thorburg ballets, a very modern affair with almost no story, and there was Pelagia, dancing again in the *corps de ballet*, wearing purple tights, a curiously patterned top in rainbow hues and a tight head-dress that quite hid her flaming hair.

Afterwards Anne and Lisa led everyone backstage and Joan and Margaret stood shyly in a corner of Mona Garland's dressing-room, trying to keep out of the way of the crowd that milled round the ballerina, now once more in her smart everyday clothes.

Pelagia came in, still in her last costume, but without the head-dress, and she was obviously pleased to the point of being over-excited.

"I never thought," Margaret whispered to Joan, "that this kind of thing would ever happen to me. It seems like a dream. I never even *saw* a ballet until the autumn."

"I'll never get used to it, either," Joan whispered back, then suddenly found herself being greeted by Johann Thorburg.

"There you are, Joan! How is the ballet coming along?"

And Joan, blushing vividly, confessed that it was progressing.

"I thought so. I've heard that you seem very busy." Then he smiled very kindly and went on to speak to Mona Garland.

When they all left by way of the stage door quite a large number of autograph hunters was waiting there. Mona Garland, of course, came in for most notice, but Joan found a book thrust under her nose.

"But I'm not – you don't want *my* autograph."

And the cold-looking girl of about seventeen answered: "You're with them. It must be wonderful. Sign it, please."

And when Joan did so, shivering in the icy wind that swept up the narrow alley-way, the girl looked at the scrawled "Joan Bradshaw" and cried triumphantly, "There! I do know you, but I didn't think you were so young. I saw your name in the programme when the students did *The Procession Passes*."

And Joan escaped from her look of hungry interest feeling strangely humbled. For the first time she really understood that the world was full of people with dull lives who haunted theatre galleries and stage doors, longing to get in touch with their idols.

The exciting evening ended with mounds of chicken sandwiches, and milky coffee for the younger ones. Pelagia and her father and mother had champagne, and Pelagia raised her glass and smiled round the living-room.

"I just had to have this to remind me that I'm really an adult."

"What did Tim say?" Anne asked.

"Oh, Tim!" Pelagia shrugged and laughed. "He said he'd been baby-snatching. He seemed quite upset."

They streamed upstairs noisily and it was midnight before everywhere was quiet.

"Those children will never get to school in time in the morning," said Mona Garland, as she stepped thankfully into bed.

But they did, with some yawns and groans, setting off as usual into the bleak early light.

Chapter Nine

Snow on the Hills

More than three weeks passed, and, though it was getting towards the end of February, the bitter weather still went on. Once or twice, briefly, there was hope of a thaw, but then the temperature would drop again and London was once more in the grip of snow and frost. The River Thames froze, the lakes in all the parks were iron-hard, and the cold was so intense that even the most restless member of the family – Anne, just then – hardly had the courage to go out at night when it was not necessary.

In their little mews house the MacAllisters were often frozen up, and things were often very difficult at the Thorburg. The house in Moone Crescent mostly continued to be warm, with plenty of running water, but when there were power cuts the heating went down and Pelagia moaned that she was never going to be really warm again.

"I think it's the end of the world," she said one afternoon, returning from the cold rehearsal rooms. "The third ice age, or whatever number it should be. We'll see polar bears roaming in all the parks before we've done."

"Oh, don't!" cried Anne, who loved animals and who suffered a good deal when she thought of their troubles.

Bonne-Bouche, who loathed the cold weather, was safe and cossetted, but the world must be full of stray dogs and cats.

Pelagia, who was just as soft-hearted, and who understood perfectly what Anne meant, said cheerfully. "Well, you needn't actually worry about polar bears, I suppose. *They're* fairly happy at the Zoo."

"But the cats, Pel. And the birds. sometimes I don't know how to bear it, the world seems so full of suffering."

"Well, it's true, no doubt, and no getting away from it. However, if you're going to agonize about anything I suppose it had better be the millions of starving children in countries suffering from drought."

"Oh, I can't even *think* of them."

Anne still had troubles far nearer home, for things were no better between her and Lisa. Lisa spent several Saturday or Sunday afternoons at the house in Moone Crescent, and on the face of it they had a pleasant time, playing records, reading and gossiping, but Joan and Margaret were often there, too, and the talk was either general or centred more on the Scott-Smithson School. The Thorburg was not often mentioned, and this, Anne was well aware, was entirely her own fault. She missed the old intimacy bitterly, but would do nothing to bring it back. Lisa was so clearly happy at the Scott-Smithson and, Anne often thought sadly, it might have been years since she left the ballet school.

Lisa did sometimes look at Anne rather wistfully, but she was put off by the barrier that Anne had half-consciously erected.

So Anne now had no real confidante. She was growing quite friendly with Helenka – in spite of the fact that there was still an element of rivalry in their relationship – and had visited her flat and met Mrs Koronov. But she had no inclination to tell Helenka the things that had slipped out naturally in the old days with Lisa. Helenka was interesting and amusing, not always the grave and vaguely tragic-looking Russian she had seemed during the previous term, and Anne loved to listen to her stories of New York, for it was a city she longed to visit. But Anne had known real, warm friendship for a long time and she was conscious of deprivation, conscious also of jealousy of Joan, who so often talked of Lisa and who seemed now to be more Lisa's friend than Anne herself.

Mona Garland, who was well aware that her middle daughter had not been very happy since Christmas, thought she knew the cause, but realized it was no use forcing Anne's confidence. The matter, it was to be hoped, would right itself, but she worried a good deal when she saw Anne looking hunched and withdrawn; not at all the cheerful girl she had once been.

Edward, too, was more withdrawn than usual from the family circle. The only boy, he might have been hopelessly spoilt, but he had early proved himself something of a solitary at home, and though he was popular at the Thorburg and had some good friends, he had certainly never been one to confide. Now he had apparently lost Tarn he was more inclined than ever to sit up in his room, working or reading.

"But he'll find another girl sooner or later, and a nicer one, I hope," his mother thought, and turned her mind towards the third problem, Delphine.

For Delphine was getting through her second term at the Thorburg in a way that was by no means quiet and retiring. After being bottom of her form two weeks running she was interviewed by the headmistress and emerged somewhat subdued. She applied herself so vigorously to her lessons the next week that her marks soared and she was third from the top, but this did not prevent her from getting into other kinds of trouble.

She and the lively Binnie thought up several pranks, not

the least of which was the mixing up of the Seniors' coats and outdoor shoes one snowy lunch-time when there was no hope of going out. Another time, when they *could* go out, they accidentally snowballed a policeman, who then promptly slipped on a hard patch of snow and fell flat on the pavement. The policeman was furious – he was young and keen on his dignity – and once more Delphine and Binnie were up before school authority.

"Delph and Binnie act as though they're the heroines of a silly school story," Carrie said ruefully to her special friends. "Really I feel *ashamed* of them."

Johann Thorburg, hearing about some of these episodes, remarked to Edwin Garland that it was to be hoped that Delphine soon learned sense.

"She's a bright child, and an attractive one, but I gather that the staff and the Seniors are up in arms. We'll give her another term and see how she goes on. I'd hate to lose her, Edwin, but sometimes it does seem as though she'd be better and happier at some stage school. She's the kind who needs to be in the limelight, and at a stage school she could get a licence at twelve and start working. It might be best for her, though I hate to say it, and, as you know, the first year is always regarded as a trial one."

Edwin Garland, horrified by this plain speaking from his old friend, gave Delphine a stern lecture, from which she emerged in very rare tears.

"Everyone is so *unfair*!" she sobbed to her unsympathetic family. "We didn't *mean* to snowball the policeman. He just got in the way."

"But you did mean to upset the Seniors, and most of the other things weren't accidents," Anne said. "We'll never get over the shame of it if they throw you out of the Thorburg. And neither would you. It might even be in the papers. 'Mona Garland's Youngest Daughter in Disgrace'."

Delphine sniffed and scowled.

"They won't throw me out. I have talent."

"Well, if having talent means that you've sunk to the bottom of your form again it doesn't get you far. You didn't stay near the top for long, did you? Remember that a dancer needs brains as well as a body!"

"I have got brains," said Delphine crossly. "But school work bores me and Binnie says –"

"Pity you ever met Binnie!"

Binnie Byrne had certainly not escaped the eye of authority and it was considered that she might not be a suitable ballet student after all.

"She has excellent technique and in many ways seems a charming child, but she isn't quite our kind," the principal ballet mistress of the School said to Johann Thorburg.

"I believe she says quite frankly that she'd have preferred to go to a stage school. But her mother wants her to be a ballerina."

They eyed each other in amused despair. the vagaries and foolishness of some mothers often made things difficult.

"We'll give *her* until July, too," said Johann Thorburg.

Though still hating the cold weather, Pelagia was perhaps the happiest of the Garlands at this time. Her ambitions soared far beyond Little Clara, but she was convinced that she would soon get her chance, and meanwhile she was enjoying the notice gained through *Casse Noisette*. Many critics had not been too enthusiastic about the production, but they had all, without exception, said that Pelagia Garland was delightful.

She saw Timothy once or twice a week and sometimes they went dancing – for Pelagia adored ballroom dancing – or else to a concert or a play. She enjoyed his company, for he was a good-looking escort and always sympathetic and understanding, except over the one subject that Pelagia wanted to avoid.

She told herself often that she didn't *want* to marry and

that Tim would get used to the idea as time went on. If he didn't then there might have to be a clean break; meantime it was quite nice to have him around. Not, of course, that she couldn't have got other admirers at the flick of an eyelash. Pelagia knew her powers, but could not often be bothered to use them.

In any case, Tim would soon have to do without her for a while. In March the Thorburg Company was going for a short provincial tour, to Edinburgh, Newcastle and Liverpool, then they were returning for two or three weeks of intensive rehearsals before setting off for the Continent. They were booked to go to Paris again, then to Barcelona and Madrid, Genoa, Milan and probably Amsterdam.

Pelagia was not looking forward to the British part of the tour, particularly if the cold weather lasted into March.

"But it's something I've got to experience," she said. "Something, I suppose, that all dancers have to take in their stride. Only I don't look forward to theatrical digs in Northern cities. Mother doesn't know she's lucky. She'll stay in all the poshest hotels and I'll be in an atmosphere of perpetual boiled cabbage and rings round the bath!"

"So was I for years," her mother pointed out mildly. "You must toughen up, Pel. Never let it be said that the present generation is soft."

"I shan't mind the simplest little *pension* in Spain or Italy. But the thought of British digs makes me quail. I can just see the hall, with a stand covered with squashy hats and umbrellas with broken spokes, and the stairs painted brown and covered with linoleum, and other people's horrid toothbrushes in the bathroom …"

"Well, I've given you some good addresses. They're clean places, with landladies who understand about dancers' needs. I can't guarantee that there won't be brown paint, though really your ideas are years out of date –"

"And vases that say 'A Present from Blackpool',"

Delphine contributed, "and maybe a poor old disgusting dog with –"

"Delph!"

"Well, I was only going to say fleas. They're not unmentionable, are they?"

"Very little is in this house, as you know. It's only that you're putting Pel off."

"I shall keep on dreaming about Spain in early May," Pelagia remarked. "Won't it be just heaven? And Paris towards the end of April will be lovely enough. Maybe the chestnut trees will just be coming into flower in the Champs-Elysées."

The stay-at-homes groaned in envy.

"I *long* to be in Paris in the spring!" Anne wailed. "Don't you want to go, Joan? I think they might take us with them. We'll need a holiday after this awful winter."

Joan laughed and nodded, but could not really imagine it. She fully intended to travel as soon as she was old enough to be in a position to pay for it herself, but those days were still far away.

"And there's a rumour," said Pelagia, with awe, "that the Company may be going to America in the late summer. New York. Think of it! And maybe Philadelphia, Washington and Boston."

"It's more than a rumour," said her mother. "It's fixed. I heard yesterday."

Pelagia gave her a starry look.

"So I shall walk down Fifth Avenue? Fly in and see that wonderful skyline? And Tim wants me to be a housewife!"

"He doesn't. He wants you to marry him and keep right on with your dancing." said Anne.

"And how long would it be before I had a dear little baby? If I married I'd *want* children, but I don't intend to marry young."

"Mother did."

"You won't influence her," said Mona Garland, with a sigh and a smile. "She'll sort it out in her own good time."

"Simple enough," Pelagia remarked. "There's no problem. I'm not getting married. I'm a dedicated type!"

Joan was happy then, too, scarcely able to believe her good fortune. For her ballet had been finished, as far as she could go, two weeks before, and she had finally dared to tell her uncle the story, and to show her designs and explain about the music she wanted.

Edwin Garland had been much impressed and had taken her sheets of beautifully painted costumes and the carefully gummed little model stages to Johann Thorburg. After a week of suspense Mr Thorburg had said that it looked extremely promising and Edwin Garland had begun to compose a suitable score out of the airs that Joan had suggested and some musical ideas of his own.

Joan, asked to go and see Johann Thorburg on Saturday morning, had been tense with excitement. It seemed incredible that she had apparently done it again and that *Farewell, Manchester* might actually be danced by the Company, might even be taken on the important continental tour.

"You see, I told you!" said Mr Thorburg, smiling warmly at her flushed, bemused face. "I knew you were capable of more good creative thought. The ballet's unusual, but not, I think, too unusual to appeal to foreign audiences. Scotland always has an appeal, somehow, and of course we'll print the story in the programme." Then he made some suggestions that Joan at once recognized as improvements and promised to do the choreography himself.

"And of course we'll pay you, my dear."

Joan's flush deepened.

"Oh, *no*! It's – it's a great honour, Mr Thorburg. I – I couldn't take anything."

"But of course you must. You've put much hard work into this ballet, and I'm always willing to pay for ideas. And what about those lovely and very clever designs? I had an expert look at them – a very distinguished man – and he said he didn't know how you'd adapted the Highland dress so well for ballet."

"It'll be a pound to speak to Joan now," Anne said, with rare sourness, when her cousin arrived back from the important interview.

"And cheap at the price," Pelagia added, rather reprovingly. She looked from Anne to the Lancashire girl who had once seemed such a hopeless outsider. "She's a very clever girl and we ought to be proud of her. I wonder who'll get the leading role?"

"Mother," suggested Delphine.

"Well, I don't know. In a new short ballet they'll probably give someone else a chance. Mother has plenty of important roles already."

"Joan ought to go to Paris to see the first night. If that's where it's to be put on."

"It's not a bit likely," said Joan and rushed off to tell Margaret the wonderful news.

Lisa telephoned on Thursday evening of the following week to ask Anne if she would like to go to her uncle's farm near Princes Risborough on Saturday.

"I've been longing to see the country in the snow and it should be all right. They're not snowed up now. The roads have been cleared, but there are still great banks and drifts of snow. There's a toboggan at the farm," Lisa went on. "We might have some fun."

"I'd love to go," Anne agreed. "If Mother says it's all right."

"And I thought I'd ask Joan and Peigi. Joan loved it when

we took her in November and Peigi has scarcely ever been out of London."

Anne's spirits immediately fell, but she wouldn't show how she felt. Clearly Lisa didn't want to be alone with her.

"I'm sure they'd like to go," she said, rather stiffly.

"Well, I thought so. We may not get another chance. But if you'd rather – Anne, listen! We'll go alone if –"

But Anne had put down the receiver and gone in search of her mother, who was ready to leave for the theatre.

"Mother, may Joan and I go to the country with Lisa on Saturday? To the farm, just for the day."

"Why, yes, I suppose so, if you don't get snowed up there. I wonder if there'll be any difficulty about trains? Some services have been badly disorganized, as you know."

"Well, it only takes a short time. I should think we'll get back somehow. If it snows much we won't go."

Anne returned to the telephone and told Lisa briefly that both she and Joan could go. Then she hung up the receiver and went to her room, where she stood biting her nails – not a habit of hers, as a rule – and really rather hating Joan. Of course it was true that they had taken Joan before, but really Lisa might ... she hadn't meant it when she suggested, too late, that they could perhaps go alone.

Joan was at first pleased to be asked to go to the farm again, for she had loved the Chiltern country on that mellow November day when she had seen it for the first time, but she began to realize that Anne was more than usually upset and finally she asked tentatively. "Would you sooner that Peigi and I didn't go to Risborough, Anne?"

And Anne scowled and said crossly, "Don't be a fool! Peigi wants to go, doesn't she? Why should I mind?"

Joan gave her a doubtful look, but left things as they were.

When they set out on Saturday morning the weather was cold, as always, but fairly bright. But as the train sped towards High Wycombe the sky clouded over and a few snowflakes began to fall. Soon they were floating down thickly and Lisa began to look worried.

"If it's going to be like this maybe we'd better not stay long. Everyone will only worry."

But the storm was a brief one, and by the time they stepped on to the platform at Princes Risborough the dark clouds had moved away, the sky was turning blue and the sun began to shine. They set off to walk towards the curving white line of the hills through a world that sparkled brilliantly, and by the time they had left the little town behind the sky was, as Lisa said, as blue as Switzerland. The middle of the lane was fairly clear, but the great banks of snow on either side were marked with purple-blue shadows and the trees were so beautiful that Joan longed to draw their feathery whiteness.

"But we can't see Whiteleaf Cross today," she said.

Anne had started the day with the determination to enjoy herself, but even in the train she had been conscious that the high spirits of the other three were genuine, while hers were not. How very friendly Lisa, Joan and Margaret seemed to have grown during the short weeks of term! They laughed and talked and made jokes, and Anne was shocked to find that many of the jokes meant nothing to her. They were peculiar to the Scott-Smithson School, and the old Thorburg jokes and references seemed forgotten between her and Lisa.

Yet, as they struggled uphill towards the farm, Lisa slipped her hand through Anne's arm and drew her a little ahead of the others.

"I can't really walk very fast, can you, Bunchy? It's so slippery and I have so many clothes on. Doesn't everywhere look heavenly? This is what I've longed for – to see the country under snow."

Anne never longed for the country, for she was a city

person through and through, but the blue-lit, sparkling curves of snow did look wonderful, and the woods were like fairyland, with each branch and twig hung with fresh snow.

"It's lovely, but it would kill me to live here."

"I don't know. My aunt loves it," Lisa remarked, looking thoughtfully at the brick and flint farm buildings that were tucked into a little valley, with the hills rising behind. "And *I* love it, too. I do know it well; all the paths through the woods and the remote hamlets and farms. I think I could adopt it."

"Oh, don't change any more!" The words slipped out, but just then Mr Gray, Lisa's uncle, came through the gate and greeted them warmly.

"I thought perhaps you wouldn't come, when the weather turned bad. But it's grand now. Except that we can't get any work done and water is such a problem."

Margaret was introduced and they all went up to the farm together, hearing about the diffculties of farm life during the bitter winter weather. Lunch followed almost as soon as they had been greeted by Mrs Gray and it was a merry meal, with even Anne telling stories of some of their own difficulties and experiences in London, and managing to make them sound funny.

Afterwards they went to get the toboggan out of the barn and climbed with it to the top of a hill field. It was a big one that would hold three at once, but not four, and Lisa, Anne and Joan made the first run because Margaret said that she wanted to look about her. She was enchanted with the Chiltern scene on that icy, brilliant afternoon.

The rush down the slope made them all shriek with excitement and for a few moments Anne felt real pleasure, even joy, as she clutched Lisa round the waist and saw the lower hedge apparently rushing towards them. But next time it was her turn to watch, and she stood against the top hedge out of the wind and once more felt left out.

"They're friends, and I'm the odd one out and Lisa doesn't *care*."

Pride then took command of her and for the rest of the short afternoon she grimly pretended to an enjoyment that she did not feel. She was glad when it was time to leave and they walked back to the station in the melancholy beauty of the winter dusk; glad when they reached London and she could at least be miserable in her own setting.

Chapter Ten

The Thorburg in Danger

On Monday Delphine had a slight cold and was kept at home, in spite of her violent protests, so Anne travelled alone. She left the Thorburg promptly at four and made her way home by Tube. She had just started to walk up Baker Street when she saw Lisa coming out of a shop.

They stared at each other and Lisa, said, "Hullo, Anne! You're early today and I'm late. I stayed at school to finish some art work and I promised Mother I'd do some shopping before going home."

"Where's Joan?" Anne asked, and Lisa looked surprised at her tone.

"Gone home ages ago, I suppose. Why?"

"Well, I should have thought she'd come shopping with you. You are rather inseparable, aren't you?"

Lisa said slowly, "She and Peigi have been very nice to me. Without them the Scott-Smithson wouldn't have been nearly so much fun. It's never very easy being a new girl when you're nearly fourteen. Anne, don't –"

"Don't what? I'm not doing anything. It's you who've deserted me. All you think about is the blessed Scott-Smithson. You –" And Anne found to her horror that all her pent-up hurt and misery was boiling over into bitter words. Much of what she said as she and Lisa walked slowly up Baker Street was not true, and she knew it, but suddenly a little devil buried deep in her made her want to hurt Lisa.

Lisa listened and tried to interpolate, but the angry words kept pouring out.

"All right, then *have* Joan and Margaret and the Scott-Smithson! It doesn't matter a bit, I know, that I'm miserable. You chose to be different, and now you *are* different, and we don't even have the same jokes any more. You aren't interested in the Thorburg –"

"Anne, will you *listen*?" Lisa cried. She rarely lost her temper, but she had one all the same, and Anne's unreasonableness and her angry face were beginning to rouse her. For Lisa had been miserable, too, held off by the barrier that her friend had erected.

"What is there to listen to? You couldn't convince me. You aren't the same girl you used to be –"

"And neither are you!" Lisa flared. "You've made things just as hard for me as you can."

"I didn't! I didn't! I tried to understand. And now you're happier with Joan and Margaret –"

"Small wonder when you do nothing but sulk and glower."

"Oh, so I sulk and glower! Then I'll leave you to finish your shopping, since my company is so unwelcome." And Anne flounced away, her eyes burning with unshed tears, a tight pain in her chest.

Lisa called, "Oh, Anne, wait!" but Anne had dived across the road and was all but running towards Moone Crescent.

She got her key out somehow and entered the house, and there, facing her on the bottom stair, was her mother. Anne, trying to keep her face hidden, flung her outdoor clothes and boots into the hall cupboard, then pushed past her mother and rushed away upstairs.

When Mona Garland followed her Anne's bedroom door was locked.

"Anne, listen! Anne, dear, what's the matter? Let me in."

"G-go away, p-please!"

"No, I won't. Do let me in."

After a few moments Anne flung open the door.

"There's no peace in this house!"

Her mother ignored the rude tone and walked quietly in, shutting the door behind her.

"Look, what's the matter? Something has upset you very much. You might tell me. I don't often try to force you, but –"

Anne sat on the bed and began to cry brokenly.

"I've quarrelled with Lisa. Really quarrelled, for the first time ever. I said some awful things, and she said a few, but not as many as me." And she poured out the ignominious story of the quarrel in Baker Street and some of the feelings that had led up to it.

Mona Garland sat on Pelagia's bed, not attempting to touch or comfort her middle daughter. She knew that she would only have been repulsed.

"Oh, Anne, you are silly! You always used to say that Lisa was like a sister, another sister. Lisa was counting on you to understand, but you've just let yourself get eaten up with jealousy."

"But she *is* happy. She's perfectly happy without me. *I'm* the one who is left out."

"Only, I'm sure, because you choose to be. Lisa isn't the kind to give up a friend just because she goes to another school. I expect she's been just as miserable as you have. You'll have to say you're sorry –"

"I will not. Never! I told her she could have Joan and Margaret and the Scott-Smithson. It's hopeless; I know it is, Mother. We'll never get right with each other again, so it's no use trying, and if you discuss it with *anyone* I'll never forgive you. Especially you mustn't mention it to Mr Thorburg."

"I won't," her mother promised. "But if you and Lisa have really quarrelled he's bound to realize it too."

"Well, let him realize it, but he's not going to interfere. It's up to Lisa. She's done nothing to try –"

"Could she? You've looked pretty grim and remote lately."

"She said I sulked and glowered. I don't. I – I hate everyone!" And Anne sobbed wretchedly.

"All this is not a bit like you. I thought you were far too sane and balanced to get so upset over something that needn't have been any kind of tragedy at all."

"I thought I was s-sane and balanced, too. I thought I was nearly grown up. I'll be fourteen very soon. I thought one s-suffered less as one grew older."

Her mother sighed and smiled.

"You'll still be saying that when you're forty."

"Shall I ever be forty? It seems quite impossible."

"Nothing's surer. Anne, you don't want to lose Lisa's friendship. You'll have to say you're sorry."

But Anne said obstinately, "It wouldn't do any good. If Lisa cares at all she'll telephone me when she gets home."

But Lisa did not telephone then or at any other time. The rest of the week passed without word from her, though Joan mentioned her sometimes. Joan knew that there had been a quarrel, for, though Lisa had not referred to it, she had shown a decided reluctance to visit the house in Moone Crescent.

"I'm going to stay away from there for a bit," was all that she had said.

So Anne was convinced that Lisa was quite happy with things as they were and she made a determined effort to cultivate her other friends, going to the cinema with

Helenka on the Saturday and to the Tate Gallery with Fernanda on Sunday afternoon. But in her deepest heart she was more unhappy than ever, and the memory of the quarrel that she had certainly instigated returned often to shame and plague her.

"Was that me?" she asked herself sometimes in the night. "Could I have been so awful?"

Then something happened that, for the time at least, drove all other thoughts out of her head. It was March, but not so very much warmer, and something had gone very badly wrong with the heating system at the Thorburg. The whole place smelt of the oil-lamps and heaters of every kind that the caretaker had produced in an attempt to heat the School, and one morning, when Anne and Delphine came round the corner into Russell Square, Delphine gave a shrill cry.

"Anne, look! There's a fire engine outside the Thorburg!"

Anne did look and her heart leaped sickeningly. There were, in fact, two fire engines, and there was a crowd outside the building, being kept back by police.

"It *couldn't* burn!" Anne gasped and raced across the road without much thought for the traffic. A bus driver hooted at her indignantly, but she didn't even notice. She was dashing round the corner of the big square, with Delphine at her heels.

The main door of the Thorburg School was open and hosepipes were lying on the steps. The crowd of casual sightseers and anxious students was growing every moment and Anne grabbed the arm of one of the Seniors.

"Oh, what is it? Is it really burning? I can't see any smoke."

"It's one of the studios at the back, I think," said the girl. "No one really seems to know. They won't let us near. They've had some difficulty over getting enough water. They say there's another engine at the back."

"There's Mr Thorburg!" cried Colin Corbett, edging his

way to Anne's side. "He looks pretty grim. Oh, if only there were something we could *do*!"

"What shall we do if the Thorburg's burnt to the ground?" Delphine asked shrilly and glared when Anne kicked her ankle.

"Shut up, can't you? It *won't* burn to the ground. It – they're bound to save it."

Anne stood there huddled into her warm coat and scarf, but cold as ice in spite of them. She looked at the two rather shabby houses that comprised the main part of the Thorburg School and remembered suddenly how scornful Joan had been when, fresh from a great northern Grammar School, she had first seen the Thorburg. It *was* shabby, but, just then, it seemed the only place on earth that was really important.

Anne found herself praying, "Oh, please, God, don't let it burn!" and she had never made a more fervent prayer in her life. If the Thorburg burned what would happen to them all? Where would they go? Would it be the end?

"No doubt they're insured," said a woman whose face was alive with excitement. "Might be a good thing. They'd get a better building for their dancing school."

"We don't want a better one!" Colin said fiercely. Anne couldn't have said a word.

Now they could see smoke rising behind the chimneys of the tall, flat-fronted houses and suddenly an acrid puff came billowing out of the front door. Anne felt sick and, seeing her form mistress, Miss Clare, pushed her way to her side.

"Oh, Miss Clare, how bad is it? Can't we do *anything*?"

Miss Clare looked pale and cold.

"I'm afraid not. No one can go near. I've just spoken to Mr Thorburg and he told me that it started in the passage that leads to the hall and studios. The nearest studio is quite badly alight. The woodwork caught and a lot of music that the caretaker put in there last night, while he was clearing out one of the storerooms. Don't look like that, Anne. It was discovered fairly soon. It's lucky that the very worst of the snow and frost have gone."

"I think I shall die if the Thorburg burns down."

Miss Clare didn't say, as someone else might have done, "Don't be dramatic, dear!" She merely shook her head and turned up her collar.

"It's a bad business. One of those oil-heaters, perhaps."

"This dreadful winter!" Anne thought. "Nothing's gone right, and now we're going to lose the Thorburg."

The whole School had now assembled and even the Juniors stood in awed silence, too upset and frightened to make nuisances of themselves. Traffic had been diverted from that side of the square and police were trying to move the crowds, but were being kind to the ballet students in their green uniform.

"Cheer up, ducks!" one young policeman said to Carrie, who was nearly in tears. "Our firemen are nearly as wonderful as our policemen! You'll be dancing again in no time."

"But it's so dreadful!" Carrie wailed.

It was an hour before the firemen began to withdraw their hoses, an hour that Anne thought she would never forget. Then Johann Thorburg and some of the teachers began to try to gather the members of the School into a group in the gardens in the centre of Russell Square. Mr Thorburg was very pale and rather dirty, for he, at last, had insisted on entering the building.

He looked at the many cold, worried faces and said clearly, "The danger is over. There is some damage, but nothing that can't be repaired, probably fairly quickly. Smoke and water haven't improved the building, but there is no real need to worry. We've been very lucky. Now I want you all to go home, but go and have hot drinks somewhere first. There's nothing at all that anyone can do here. Go home and practise if you can, or else get on with your school work, and at nine o'clock in the morning I want everyone to assemble at the Thorburg Theatre. I'll put a notice on the front door in case everyone isn't here."

Anne, Helenka, Fernanda, Colin and one or two other boys trailed unhappily away to the nearest coffee-bar and were soon joined by as many students as could pack themselves in. Most people talked a great deal, but Anne was still sunk into the horror of the recent experience. If she had needed anything to convince her of the importance of the Thorburg in her life the fire had certainly done it. Her prayer had been answered and the School had not burned to the ground, but she knew that she would be haunted for some time.

She went home with Helenka to Bloomsbury Street, since she dreaded returning to Moone Crescent, where everyone would be out. And it was only when they were half-way through lunch that she remembered Delphine.

"I forgot her! How could I?"

"Oh, she'll be all right," Helenka said calmly. "That child can look after herself."

"I know she can, and the worst of the bad weather is over, thank goodness. Mother made me stick to her like glue while travelling was so difficult. All the same I ought not to have forgotten her. I wonder if she went home? Annali and Rosa will be there, of course, but Mother was going out to lunch after her class and Pel has a rehearsal and will probably only have sandwiches. I expect Ed went off somewhere."

Anne went home soon after the meal and found that she was the first, but Edward arrived soon afterwards, with Delphine not far behind. She had been home to lunch with Binnie Byrne and was still agog over the fire.

"Wasn't it exciting, Anne? Oh, of course I know it was awful, too, but it *was* insured and we'd have got somewhere else."

"You have no feeling for tradition at *all*!" said Anne scathingly. "I don't know how you *can* talk like that and you a Garland. Oh, come and practise. I suppose we've got to do something."

They changed into their practice clothes and, joined by Edward, were soon working hard in the studio. The familiar exercises comforted and soothed Anne, as always, but it was a very strange and uncomfortable day and she longed for it to be over.

Chapter Eleven

"Will spring never come?"

Pelagia, of course, had heard about the fire before the rehearsal was over and had even been privileged to go with her father (who happened to call in at the rehearsal rooms about something) and Johann Thorburg to see the damage.

"It looked terrible," she told her assembled family, when they gathered in the living-room late that afternoon. "Water everywhere and a ghastly smoky smell, but it really might have been worse."

"It might have been much worse," said Edwin Garland. "Johann thinks that it won't take long to get back almost to normal, though that one studio will have to be partly rebuilt. Meanwhile it's going to be difficult for everyone: a grand reorganization job. But he'll tell the whole school about it in the theatre tomorrow. Some of the ballet classes will be held in the rehearsal rooms for the time being. He hopes that school lessons may be resumed in a day or two, as the classrooms weren't damaged. But a lot of water ran down into the cloakrooms."

"Oh, Father, you didn't see it burning!" cried Anne.

He glanced sympathetically at her pale face.

"It must have been awful. But cheer up! Things aren't really too bad."

"But – but it shakes you. If the Thorburg could burn then almost anything could happen."

"Well, that's true," her father agreed, for he saw no point in trying to gloss over the dangers of life. "Anything *can* happen, but this time disaster was averted."

"I shall never feel safe again." And then Anne glanced at Joan, who had been listening in silence. "I suppose *you* think it's a fuss about nothing?"

Joan went red. Anne was being very unfriendly these days and there seemed nothing much that she could do about it.

"Of course I don't. I think fire is always frightening and I know just what the Thorburg means to you all."

"Yes, but you once said –"

But Pelagia, tactful for once, chipped in, "So now we're going to have everyone at the rehearsal rooms and I must say that'll be jolly! It's lucky we haven't got anything much on this week, but we've got our own classes –" Then she sighed and stretched. "Oh, roll on April and Paris! Sometimes it seems as though spring will never come. Life does seem dismal at the moment. But it's true what Father says. That particular agony is over, so we needn't look as though there's been a death in the family."

But the burning of the Thorburg had another direct effect on the Garland family. Things were soon organized so that different classes went to the rehearsal rooms at a set time every morning. The junior classes went at nine o'clock and the livelier spirits amongst them enjoyed the change of enviroment, dashing noisily up the dark old stairs and exploring hidden corners of the building when they got the chance.

Delphine and Binnie Byrne were the leading pair, of course, and the caretaker soon learned to dislike them. He called Delphine "that ginger-haired young devil" and wasn't in the least impressed when he learned that the "young devil" was a Garland and didn't regard herself as ginger-haired.

"My hair is a beautiful red," said Delphine, posturing in front of one of the spotted old mirrors in a changing-room. She and Binnie had arrived early and it was a mistake on the caretaker's part that they were in the building at all. He had left the door open while he slipped out for a morning paper and had found them poking their noses into the office.

Driven out of the office, and still in the building only by good luck and the fact that the telephone had rung, they soon tired of the changing-room and crept out to explore further. Already the members of their class could be heard arriving and the ballet mistress could not be far away.

It was Binnie who found the open window – it was a warmer morning than for a very long time – and looked out to see a narrow stretch of flat roof.

"I say, Delph! Let's just climb out there!"

Already in their practice clothes, they hopped out cheerfully and Binnie walked unconcernedly to the edge of the roof, which was only at first floor level. At the end of the roof a high, foot-wide wall extended to the next building, dividing two grim backyards.

Binnie looked at it thoughtfully and put out a tentative foot.

"I always fancied myself as a tightrope walker!"

"It's a lot wider than a tightrope," said Delphine, doing an arabesque rather near the edge of the roof. "Rather a wide wall, really, I could walk it easily."

"It's quite a drop. You'd better not."

"Pooh! I'm not afraid. I have wonderful balance."

"You're an awful show-off, as the others are always saying," said Binnie amiably. "All right. I dare you!"

"Done!" said Delphine cheerfully and stepped on to the top of the wall.

It was true that she had excellent balance and all might have been well if the caretaker had not, at the moment when she reached the middle, looked out of the window and given an irate shout. Startled, Delphine glanced round and then somehow missed her footing. Her shriek of fright was echoed by Binnie as she plunged down into the yard on the right, crashing against a dust-bin.

Delphine herself knew nothing of what followed. She never heard or saw the ballet mistress, Miss Tindall, who was the first to reach the yard and the crumpled little figure with tumbled red curls. She never heard Binnie's wails of guilt and terror, nor the voluble indignation and fright of the unfortunate caretaker.

Miss Tindall, a young woman with plenty of common sense and a wide knowledge of the human body, moved Delphine only enough to get her lying flat, there in the dreary yard. And she remained crouching by the child until an ambulance was somehow manoeuvred near to the back door and men appeared with a stretcher. Then, knowing that efforts were being made to contact Delphine's father and mother, she herself went with her to the hospital.

Meanwhile, Mr Thorburg had arrived at the rehearsal rooms, looking rather more than his age. Delphine had been a trial to everyone, but she was a lovable little thing in spite of all the trouble she had caused and quite likely to turn into a promising dancer. She was the adored youngest child of his greatest friends. Apart from all that, she was the responsibility of the Thorburg School and he was shocked beyond measure that such a thing could have happened.

The caretaker, practically in tears, told his story. It hadn't been his fault. How was he to know that the young dev – the young ones would creep in when he had just slipped out to buy a newspaper? Well, he had been going to turn them out again, naturally, but then the telephone had rung and he had answered it. Heaven knew he didn't wish harm to anyone ... it was a terrible, tragic thing ... but it wasn't his fault, and no one could ever say it was.

The whining cockney voice went on and on and eventually Johann Thorburg cut him off abruptly.

"All right. The window was open and they climbed out and did that silly, dangerous thing. There's really nothing more to say at the moment. We don't know how badly the child is hurt. Her parents have gone to the hospital and we can only wait until there's some news. Pull yourself together, man. It was an accident."

Classes, according to his orders, were going on. The work of the school couldn't stop because Delphine Garland was injured, and it was, in any case, the only way to keep the upset and over-excited Juniors in order. Someone had taken over from Miss Tindall, but she soon returned, saying there had been no news when she left.

"But where's the other child? Binnie?" Johann Thorburg asked.

"In class, I think. I sent orders that she was to carry on as usual. Someone said she was hysterical and I thought it was the best way to calm her. I couldn't leave Delphine."

But Binnie was not in class, she was crouching in a corner of the cloakroom, watched over by a young, much disturbed member of the *corps de ballet*. Mr Thorburg dismissed the girl and raised Binnie to her feet. A more wretchedly unhappy child he had rarely seen and his warm heart went out to her.

"Binnie, my dear! It was an accident, wasn't it? Try to tell me exactly what happened, and then I'll telephone your mother and you must go home."

Binnie wailed anew, hiccoughing and sobbing.

"I d-dared her. If she's dead it's all my fault. I'll have k-killed her!"

"You dared her to walk on the wall? But why?"

Binnie gasped out the little story of how they had climbed out of the window.

"I d-did tell her she'd b-better not, at first. The, she b-boasted. Delph was always boasting. So then I s-said –" More hiccoughs. "The c-caretaker shouted and she looked round and f-fell, but if I'd never d-dared her. – Oh, Mr Thorburg, if she's d-dead what shall I do?"

"She isn't dead. We do know that." And he comforted her as best he could, then telephoned her mother, whom fortunately he found at home, and sent her off in a taxi, a small, sodden figure, infinitely pathetic.

Delphine returned to consciousness in a hospital private room, with her father and mother sitting on either side of the bed.

"I fell," said Delphine, in a vague, muzzy voice. "It wasn't Binnie's fault."

"Never mind whose fault it was," Mona Garland said gently.

"What time is it? Where am I? Ow! I hurt!"

"It's nearly lunch-time and you're in hospital. You'll be all right, darling. Just go to sleep."

A nurse came in then and gave the child an injection. Her parents looked at each other over the small, prone figure and then left quietly, making their way to the waiting-room, where Pelagia was looking white and uneasy.

"How is she? Did she come round?"

"Yes," her father told her. "And now she's going to sleep. We saw the specialist just before we went in to her. He says it's really too early to tell. There's some damage to her spine; very badly bruised. And she has slight concussion."

"Her *spine*?" repeated Pelagia, and looked sick. She could not, however, say the words that were ringing through her head. "A dancer's spine ... Delph!"

"How *could* she be such a little idiot!" she cried finally.

"Miss Tindall blames herself. She was a little late, owing

to a slight traffic hold-up. Binnie and Delph were early and managed to get in, though the caretaker had had strict orders not to let anyone in until a member of the staff was present."

"But Delph is ten. She ought to have enough sense not to act the goat because she's alone for a few minutes. I'd be inclined to blame that Binnie."

"Binnie's gone home, broken-hearted. And almost the only thing Delph said was that it wasn't Binnie's fault. It's no good blaming anyone." For once Mona Garland looked every year of her age and a good many more. She had never known a worse morning than the one that had just passed, and yet she would have to dance Aurora in *The Sleeping Beauty* that evening, looking lovely and assured, as though her youngest child was not lying with an injured spine.

Edward and Anne were not told until the end of the afternoon, for the Juniors who knew about the accident had been sworn to secrecy and were all so frightened and upset that they obeyed without difficulty.

"They can't do anything to help," Johann Thorburg had said. "They're better getting on with their work, rather than moping at home."

It was the headmistress, Miss Shane, who told them. Edward took it quietly, though he went very white, but Anne was loud in her fright and despair.

"But, Miss Shane, we ought to have been told earlier. This morning ... But where is she? She isn't *dead*?"

"Far from it," said Miss Shane, looking at her with deepest sympathy. "She has slight concussion, but she came round and spoke to your father and mother. She's sleeping now, but I expect you can both see her tomorrow. There was nothing you could do, dear."

"But you said she was injured. She fell from the top of a wall. It isn't *only* concusssion?"

"She has bruised her spine," said Miss Shane, with

reluctance. She much disliked her task, but accepted it as part of her responsibility. "No, don't look like that. It may not be anything very serious."

"Delph!" cried Anne. "Delph, who is always talking about being a ballerina!"

"She will be yet. Honestly, Anne, I spoke to your father and he told me that the specialist, who is a very eminent man, admitted that it is too early to tell, but he is fairly sure it won't be anything very serious. She won't dance for a time, but she'll certainly dance again. You must believe that."

Anne and Edward went home together in a taxi. Anne absolutely refused to take any slower mode of transport. And as they drove along Marylebone Road she said drearily, "Everything is going wrong, Ed. The Garlands always used to seem so lucky and secure. It's as I said after the fire. Nothing's safe. Anything could happen. But I never thought it would happen to Delph."

"She'll be all right; she's bound to be," said Edward, who just had to believe it. Delphine often irritated him, but the thought of her lying in a hospital bed was almost unbearable.

Anne stared out at the bleak afternoon. The morning's faint promise of warmth had not lasted, and now it was cold and grey again, with no trace of spring.

"Will spring ever come, do you think?"

She had thought that she could not be much more miserable. Lisa had neither telephoned or written and, though Anne had tried to forget the quarrel and to resign herself to the fact that she had lost her friend, she had never really succeeded. In two days it would be her birthday and she had pinned all her hopes on that. Now, driving through London, nothing seemed important but what had happened to Delphine.

Anne and Edward got out of the taxi just as Joan was

using her key at the front door. They all gathered in the living-room and were joined by Annali and Rosa, who thought themselves part of the family. Joan was desperately shocked by the news, for she had grown fond of her troublesome little cousin and she knew – as well as everyone else – the unspoken thought that was present in the room: "How will it affect Delphine's dancing?"

"The lucky ones," said Anne bitterly, later, "are Father, Mother and Pel, who *have* to go out and behave as usual. I don't see how we're to settle to anything."

"We'd better do our homework," Edward said, without enthusiasm.

"It's Friday. We've got the whole weekend."

Just then Mona Garland came downstairs, ready to leave for the theatre. She looked at the miserable faces of Edward, Anne and Joan and said abruptly, "You'd better all come along to the Thorburg. You can watch from the wings. It will be a new experience for Joan."

Edward refused, saying that he thought he would go over and see Jocheli, but Anne and Joan ran to get their coats. Anything was better than spending the evening in uneasy waiting.

As they were leaving Edwin Garland said, "I've just telephoned the hospital. She's sleeping peacefully. They seem very hopeful about her."

So a little of the nightmare feeling of disaster lifted, and Anne roused herself enough to talk to Joan as they followed the two adults through the stage door.

"Doesn't it seem a long time since I brought you here for the first time? I suppose it doesn't feel so strange now?"

Joan sniffed the dusty, stuffy air and shook her head.

"Not quite so strange. I see what you meant about the exciting smell. Then I just thought it was rather unpleasant. I *never* thought I'd get to know the backstage regions of a theatre."

They sat in Mona Garland's dressing-room until "Overture Beginners", then Anne led the way to the OP corner.

"Mother isn't on, of course, during the Prologue. You know that, don't you? You saw *The Sleeping Beauty* at Covent Garden. A far grander production than this, of course. We shan't be in the way here."

And Joan, remembering that wonderful night when she and Margaret had first gone to Covent Garden, crouched there beside Anne, marvelling at the strangeness of seeing the ballet from such a different angle. If she leaned forward she could just glimpse a corner of the auditorium, and she could see almost the whole of the stage, where the Court was now assembling to the familiar music. The brilliantly dressed figures passed very close to her, but now she was not surprised to find that some of the costumes looked garish and even scruffy when seen at close range.

It was all very exciting and interesting and for a time she even forgot poor, suffering Delphine, but during the first interval Anne said, "I wonder if Delph is awake now? Mother said they'd go and see her on the way home, but I suppose we'll have to wait in the car. Oh, Joan, sometimes it comes over me in a wave of horror. Mostly I can hardly believe it."

"It's awful for Aunt Mona having to dance," said Joan, as they ducked out of the way of the electricians and other busy people.

Yet when Mona Garland appeared on stage she looked, as always, a young, eager girl, thrilled because it was her birthday. The Rose Adagio was so perfect that Joan caught her breath in wonder and incredulity. This thing that happened whenever a great dancer showed all her powers of feeling and technique was something that always seemed a kind of miracle. Far away were the days when she had thought the life of a dancer drudgery. Hard work there was in

plenty, but when the endless hours at the *barre* resulted in something so perfect, then it was all worthwhile, both for the dancer and for the audience.

Delphine was awake when her parents saw her briefly that night, and everyone was as hopeful as possible.

"Of course it *is* too early to tell," said Edwin Garland, when they rejoined the anxious girls in the car. "But I feel she'll be all right. So get a good night's sleep and you can see her tomorrow afternoon."

When they reached home Annali, who was waiting with sandwiches and coffee, said to Anne, "Lisa rang up. She says she'll wait up until you ring her back."

Anne gave her a startled look.

"I'll go and telephone her, then."

With a fast-beating heart she went to the extension in the study, where she would not be overheard. Lisa herself answered and her voice sounded shy and breathless.

"Oh, Anne, Annali said you'd gone to the Thorburg. I – I just wanted to say how dreadfully sorry I am about Delphine. F-Father told me when I got home from school."

"It's been awful," said Anne, conscious of tears near the surface. It was so long since she had heard Lisa's voice, and she was desperately anxious not to say the wrong thing. "Her spine ... we've been trying not to think of it. But Father seems more cheerful. They've just been in to see her."

"I – I had to speak to you. I wanted to ages ago, really. I'll go and visit her when they'll let me. Anne – are you all right?"

"I'll live," said Anne, but her voice shook. "Thank you for ringing, Lisa. I'll tell you when there's any news."

"She didn't ring until she just had to," she told herself, as she walked slowly back to the living-room. "But I'm glad she did. Oh, I wonder if we'll *ever* be really friends again?"

Chapter Twelve
The Thorburg on Tour

Anne's fourteenth birthday, which fell on a Sunday, passed quietly. She got a great many presents and was promised a special treat as soon as things settled down, but just then she didn't mind about parties or treats. Lisa walked across the park with a present and they met face to face for the first time since the quarrel, both rather shy and restrained. But at least Lisa had come, and, as the news about Delphine grew better, Anne's spirits improved.

By the time she had been in hospital for a week Delphine was a by-word with the nurses, who found her alternately enchanting and quite maddening. She would drive them nearly silly with her moods and demands, and then turn on the charm and have them eating out of her hand.

One nurse, inclined to be sentimental, called her "the little dancer", and most of them were fascinated by Mona Garland and Delphine's red-haired brother and sisters.

"I call them a lovely family," said the sentimental one.

Delphine was even in the London papers, for the news got around that Mona Garland's youngest daughter had had an accident. Both the *News* and the *Standard* published paragraphs about her, and the *Standard* also carried a photograph of Delphine in bed, with her mascot on the pillow.

"She'll be worse than ever when she comes home," Edward said ruefully, but they were all wildly relieved by the good news that presently came from the hospital. Delphine would have to rest for at least two weeks more and then would have to have various kinds of treatment, but there was little doubt that she would be back at the Thorburg School after Easter. Perhaps not dancing much at first, but that, said the great specialist, would come.

As soon as she could have plenty of visitors a great many of her friends found their way to her room, including Binnie, who was at first very subdued. But she soon cheered up when she found that Delphine didn't blame her, and they made so much noise that one of the Sisters had to quieten them for the sake of the patient next door.

Johann Thorburg visited her, and even such august people as William Royal and Barbary Brown, and Delphine thrived under the attention.

Anne, who sometimes slipped into the hospital after school, went cheerfully one day and was horrified to be met by a grave-faced Sister.

"I'm glad you've come, dear. We none of us can get anything out of her. She's terribly upset about something. I telephoned your home, but your father and mother were out."

Anne opened the door and at first couldn't see Delphine at all, then spied the top of her head. Delphine was half-buried under the bedclothes and eventually raised a blotched and ravaged face.

"But, Delph *dear*, what's the matter? Do you feel ill again?"

Delphine stared at her with great greenish eyes.

"No, I d-don't feel ill, but I wish I'd *died*!"

"But, Delph, that's silly. You're getting better. You're

going to get up soon. What on earth *is* it?" Anne was appalled and very frightened. Never had she seen her young sister looking so tense and fragile.

"I think you should have told me. After all, I'm the one who has to bear it. I never thought ... I never dreamed, but I know it must be true."

"What? I don't in the least understand. If you're going to get so worked up I'd better fetch Sister."

Anne started to sit down by the bed and her foot touched something hard. She bent down and picked up a book, a bright new edition of *What Katy Did*. Anne had read it, but years ago, and for a moment the significance of it didn't strike her. But Delphine flinched back from the sight of the book.

"Someone brought me that. I – I started to read it. She fell out of a swing and she lay in a dreadful dreary room and she couldn't walk. And then I knew that I'd be the same and that no one had d-dared to tell me. That's why William Royal and everyone have been so kind. I'll never w-walk or d-dance again."

"Well, I don't know who the idiot was who brought you a book about that," Anne said fiercely. She dropped the book and took her sister's hot hand. "Don't be a fool, love. *You're* not Katy. Besides, she did walk in the end, and did a lot of other things."

Delphine stared at her.

"You mean there never was any danger that I couldn't dance?"

Anne hesitated, remembering the days of almost unspoken fear.

"Not much. We never mentioned it, anyway. But now Mr Sheen-Brown says definitely that you'll be as good as new and quite soon."

"They haven't told you the truth," said Delphine, in a suddenly quiet and strangely adult voice.

"But I'm sure they have. I'm going to fetch Sister."

The Sister listened to Anne's tale, then said briskly, "Mr Sheen-Brown is in the hospital. I'll get hold of him and ask him if he'll have a word with Delphine. Of course she'll dance again."

The specialist came promptly and was alone with Delphine for nearly ten minutes. He came out smiling and said to Anne, who was hovering anxiously, "Poor kid! She seems to be convinced now. I'm sorry this should have happened."

Delphine looked like a slightly sodden angel when Anne went back. The look of strain and fear had gone from her face.

"He's nice. He says I've got too much imagination and it will definitely be all right. But gosh! It was awful! Two hours of thinking I was going to be – to be a helpless invalid. And then I knew that I couldn't bear not to dance." She looked up at Anne earnestly. "I'll be different. I will, really. I'll work and be sensible."

Anne, deeply moved, looked down at her.

"Oh, Delph, *dear*! You *do* sound Katyish now. Like an old-fashioned story-book child. It's horribly like a death-bed conversion."

Delphine chuckled and looked much more like her usual self.

"OK. I'm converted. You'll see."

"That'll be the day! Saint Delphine. The Thorburg will be amazed."

"I mean it, though. I really do."

A nurse appeared then with tea for both of them, and Anne talked lightly while they ate and drank. Then she kissed Delphine awkwardly and walked out into the open air. Almost, it seemed, she had been far away from London and suddenly returned. It was a grey March day, but the scene suddenly burst on Anne with a strange feeling of newness. She walked over into the middle of Trafalgar Square and stood near one of the fountains, slowly rotating, so that she could look each way in turn. The National Gallery ... St Martin's ... Whitehall ... Admiralty Arch. The endless red buses as the rush hour got under way ... the grey wings of the pigeons.

"London!" she said, half-aloud. "It's real. We're real. And Delph, poor Delph, shut away in there, thinking she'd never dance again."

She told the story to her mother, but not to anyone else. Delphine might do that herself one day, for her natural feeling for the dramatic would probably make it impossible for her to keep it to herself.

"I felt so awful, Mother. She looked such a tragic scrap. But she's quite all right now. Mr Sheen-Brown talked to her."

"Oh, dear! What an awful thing to happen," said her mother. "That poor child, and poor you, Anne. But you seem to have handled it very sensibly."

"It shook me, though. I've never seen Delph like that."

But the next day Delphine was her old self, imperious and showing off. And quite soon Anne had almost forgotten the "death-bed conversion".

During all the cold and dreary weeks Timothy Blandford had been more often unhappy than happy. Of course he could see Pelagia dance whenever he wished, and he now knew most of the staff at the Thorburg Theatre, and sometimes she went out with him for a late meal afer a performance. But more often she only wanted to get home, saying that she was tired and frozen stiff. Occasionally they went to a cinema and these were some of Timothy's happiest times, because he could concentrate on Pelagia beside him (certainly not on the film). Sometimes she let him hold her hand, and when she was very tired she even leaned cosily against him. Very occasionally, when they were alone, she would let him kiss her, and even kissed him back, but she would never be serious over the big question that was always in Timothy's mind.

As the weather grew a little better Pelagia became progressively more lively and sometimes she could make him laugh helplessly, for she had quite a wit when it suited her. Often he realized the strange power of Pelagia, as Joan had recognized it on that afternoon when she read poetry.

He had known her now for about six months, which some people might not have thought very long, but Timothy had been convinced during every moment of that time that he had found the only girl he would ever wish to marry.

And, now that it was March, he was desperately conscious that soon she would be going away, first to the North and then, after two or three weeks back in London, abroad for quite a long time. He felt that he wouldn't mind so much if only they fully understood each other; if Pelagia would promise to marry him next year, or even the year after – though naturally it would have been better if she would have agreed to marry him then there.

But Pelagia was excited about the coming Continental tour and curious, but slightly rueful, about the visits to Edinburgh, Newcastle and Liverpool.

"Edinburgh's lovely, I know, but so much livelier and warmer at Festival time. I don't know why we have to go now. It's sure to be freezing."

"I'll fly up and see you at the weekend," the young man offered, and Pelagia shrugged and laughed.

"Oh, Tim, I shouldn't. It's such a waste of good money, and, besides, there won't *be* much weekend. We'll be moving south again to Newcastle on Sunday morning."

"I could come on the overnight train, then, on the Friday I could see you on Saturday morning and go to both performances, if you're dancing each time."

"I shouldn't," Pelagia said again. "Oh, Tim, you'd better find some other girl. I'm no good to you."

But Timothy assured her passionately that he would never want another girl.

This conversation took place a week or two before the Company was to go north, and no one but the two concerned knew about it; but a few nights later Pelagia arrived home last and burst into the living-room, where her parents were just finishing their coffee and sandwiches. Her cheeks were very pink and she looked worked up and vaguely defiant.

"Did Tim bring you home? Why didn't you ask him in?" her mother asked.

Pelagia flopped down and began to wolf the remaining sandwiches.

"I came in a taxi by myself. I wouldn't let Tim bring me. I've finished with him. I told him so, and this time he believed me."

They eyed her cautiously.

"But why?" her father asked. "He's a fine young man. Sensible except where you're con –" he stopped abruptly, but Pelagia took up the words.

"Of course he never *has* been sensible over me. He fell in love that first day in the Tower and he's been bothering ever since. I've told him and told him that I don't mean to marry, but tonight he asked me again. He said he must have an answer, so I gave him one. I said no. I don't *want* to marry, though I do like him. I just want to dance and travel and try and find out where I'm going."

"You'll miss him," said Mona Garland.

Pelagia helped herself to another cup of milky coffee.

"Maybe. I don't mind being admired, and I love going dancing with him, and he's always been so kind and understanding when I'm fed up or things go wrong. But it isn't fair to keep him hanging about when I *know* I won't marry him. Now is it?"

"Well, not if you're sure."

"Yes, I'm sure," said Pelagia.

Timothy sought Mona Garland out at the Thorburg Theatre on a night when Pelagia was not dancing. He looked, she thought, older and sterner than ever before, but there was not much comfort she could give him.

"I think she does mean it now, Tim. She's only eighteen and in some ways she's young for her age."

"You don't think there's anyone else? I've never dared to ask her that."

"No, I'm sure there's no one. She just thinks she wants to be free, and just now she can think of nothing but going abroad in April and presently getting some hot sunshine. You know how she adores the sun."

"She could still enjoy the sun and be engaged to me," said Timothy glumly.

"So she could, but I'd leave her alone for quite a time. Maybe until she comes home from the Continental tour. It's the only way. Edwin and I are very sorry about it, if that's any consolation to you. We'd like you for a son-in-law."

And Timothy looked at the beautiful woman before him, whom he had so luckily managed to see alone, though there were always people clamouring to see her after a performance, and saw in her something of Pelagia, though a Pelagia grown graver and more mature.

"She sent me packing. She doesn't want me. But of course I'll wait. I may be a fool, but I'll wait as long as there's any hope."

"Let her go for now. Let her see if she really likes freedom."

At home, once the rest of the family knew about her decision, Pelagia was airy and casual.

"Poor Tim! It's hard on him, but I always said I'd have to do it."

"You must be mad," Anne said frankly. "I wouldn't mind marrying him myself."

"Just sensible," said Pelagia.

"But he's *gorgeous!*" Delphine chipped in. She had arrived home a few days before, and, though she still had to go to the hospital frequently for treatment and rest a good deal, she was making rapid progress and was delighted with her new importance in the household. Just now Bonne-Bouche was sitting on her stomach, as she usurped Pelagia's old place on the sofa. "He came to see me and brought heavenly chocolates, and the nurses were just crazy about him."

"Well, he can wait until you or Anne grows up," Pelagia said lightly. "One redheaded Garland is probably much like another."

"They're not like you," Joan said unexpectedly, and then blushed under Pelagia's amused stare. "Well, they're not," she insisted. "Not Anne, and not Delph, really."

Pelagia laughed and half-danced out of the room, then went rushing upstairs to get on with her packing.

Of course both Edwin and Mona Garland were going on tour, too, and they certainly wished that this time they could stay at home, for neither liked leaving Delphine, though Annali had looked after the child like a second mother all her life, and was perfectly capable – or at least as capable as anyone else – of keeping her in order and taking her to the hospital when required.

"Sometimes I think I'll retire," Mona Garland said to her husband, and he sighed and laughed.

"My dear, you mustn't think of it. Not for at least five years, anyway. Johann would have a fit, and so would your public."

"All the same, there are times when I get tired of the life. And one thing I'm determined about – we're going to take all the children to Paris after Easter. Joan *ought* to go, as they're doing her ballet, and the others all need a holiday after this wretched winter and all the trouble there's been. Anne still isn't her old self, and poor Delph is so pale."

Edwin Garland agreeing, the news was broken to the younger ones that evening. Joan was incredulous and Anne, Edward and Delphine wildly pleased.

"I knew we'd go!" Anne cried. "Oh, it will be wonderful to see Paris in the spring!"

Joan rushed away as soon as she could to tell Margaret, for it really seemed like a miracle that she was to see a foreign city. And the atmosphere remained cheerful at the house in Moone Crescent until the travellers left for Edinburgh.

Edinburgh *was* cold, but lovely in its ancient grey dignity, and in ordinary circumstances Pelagia would probably have been perfectly happy. But as the train sped north her cheerfulness had dropped off her and could not be retrieved. It was because Timothy had not been there to see her off, she thought vaguely. He had not written or telephoned, either, and that wasn't like Tim, who had always been so persistent.

She walked along Princes Street alone and, for almost the first time in her life, lonely, and every time she glanced at the long frieze of the Old Town on its hill, ending with the Castle on its rock, something struck at her heart.

She need not have been alone; there were plenty of people in the *corps de ballet* who would have been glad of her company. But she continued to go out for solitary walks. One afternoon she climbed Arthur's Seat and looked down at the Palace of Holyroodhouse and the whole of the city outspread and did not even notice that the wind was cold. She was absorbed in her rather dismal thoughts, trying, without success, to work things out.

"I *don't* want to marry. It's true. I always thought I'd have to throw Tim over. Then why do I feel like this? Why doesn't he write? Perhaps he'll come up at the weekend as he said."

Edinburgh liked the Thorburg Company and every performance was well booked. Pelagia continued to be an enchanting Little Clara and sometimes startled the people waiting at the stage door when they realized that she was grown up and not a child.

Mona Garland saw little of her daughter, but she did realize that Pelagia seemed unusully thoughtful and aloof and once she asked, "Are the digs all right, Pel? Mrs Cameron is a bit of an old dragon, but she cooks well."

"They're fine," Pelagia said vaguely. "A bit Calvinistic, if you know what I mean. Mrs C seems to set great store by the sabbath, but it doesn't bother me."

"Well, come back with us to our hotel tonight after the show."

Pelagia went, stepping with equal vagueness into the atmosphere of peace and luxury.

"It must be nice to be important," she said to her mother, giving the waiter such an absent-minded, wholly enchanting smile that he nearly dropped the tray. "But I'm right enough where I am. People in the *corps* don't expect luxury. I even feel slightly guilty being here."

"Oh, rubbish!" said her mother, puzzled by her air of not being quite present. It was to be hoped that Pelagia was missing Timothy, but she had never mentioned him once. It might be, of course, that she had fallen in love with someone else, but, mentally going over the male members of the Company, Mona Garland couldn't think whom it might be.

Timothy didn't appear and they went south to Newcastle, where poor Pelagia had one of the worst experiences of her ballet career. She got hiccoughs during the party scene of *Casse Noisette* and spent the interval frantically trying every suggested remedy. Thinking herself cured, she walked on stage with the Nutcracker Prince at the start of the Kingdom of Sweets act and immediately gave another vast uncontrolled hiccough. Probably the music drowned the sound of it, but Pelagia was stiff with horror, and she spent the rest of the time, when she was supposed to be looking so delighted and interested, fighting off more trouble, holding her breath until she thought she would burst. And right at the end, when she was taking that final curtain with her mother and William Royal, the worst happened and the audience laughed.

"I wish I were *dead*!" wailed Pelagia, in the dressing-room. "I'll never live down the shame of it. Never!"

"Oh, cheer up!" said an older member of the *corps*. "Worse than that can happen. Think if it had been *Les Sylphides*. I once had an absolutely unending fit of sneezing just at the most soulful part. It was frightful."

"But they *laughed*!"

"Well, never mind. They'll soon forget."

"I shan't, though," groaned Pelagia, and she went gloomily back to her digs, aware that, if it had happened in London, Timothy might have been there to comfort her.

It was April when they reached Liverpool, but the wind blew coldly off the River Mersey and bits of paper were being blown about the streets. Pelagia thought it a dreary city, even though the audiences were enthusiastic and kind, and she began to long passionately to be back in London. Perhaps then she would see Timothy, and soon it would be time to go away to the sun. Not that it would be very hot in Paris in late April, but then would come Spain.

"And I can't possibly be miserable in Spain, even if Tim doesn't come back," Pelagia said to herself, as she pushed her way up Church Street through the slow-moving afternoon shoppers. "All I *really* need is some hot sunshine and blue skies. That's all that's the matter with me."

Chapter Thirteen
Springtime in Paris

Meanwhile, the stay-at-homes thought often of Paris while coping with their everyday lives. Joan had taken a pile of books out of the library and bought a Paris street map, and sometimes her heart seemed to leap with excitement at the thought of what was to come. The scenery for her ballet was being painted in the Thorburg workshop and rehearsals would start just as soon as the Company returned to London. It all seemed so wonderful that there were times when she could hardly believe in her good fortune.

But London still had magic and, once the bad weather had given place to the first small green buds and a few crocuses in the squares and parks, she and Margaret continued their long interrupted exploration of the city. Sometimes Lisa went with them, and was able to show them much that they might otherwise not have discovered, but often they went alone, wandering round squares and gardens in many different districts, exploring the City on Sunday afternoons, seeing the old churches and feeling great triumph when some unexpected treasure was revealed to them.

"Paris *and* London!" Joan marvelled one day, as they

strolled past the Old Bailey. "Oh, I wish you were coming, too, Peigi. It's the only thing that spoils it."

"But you'll have Anne. And Edward and Delphine as well, I suppose."

"Anne isn't very friendly. She hasn't been for most of this term. I know she blames me because of Lisa, but we had to be nice to her, and I *like* Lisa."

"So do I," Margaret agreed. "It's silly of Anne to be jealous. I don't see why we can't all be friends."

"Neither do I. It would be far nicer. She and Lisa do see each other again now, but I don't think they're quite as they were before. I don't know what Anne said during that quarrel, but I think it must have been something pretty bad. Lisa was terribly miserable for a long time."

It was true that Anne and Lisa were meeting, but also true, as Joan surmised, that they had never got back their old easy friendship. The quarrel had never been mentioned between them, and, in her secret heart, Anne knew that all could not be well until it was and she apologized. But somehow she couldn't do it, and the weeks drifted by. Things had almost gone back to normal at the Thorburg School and everyone was working very hard. There was not really much time for brooding.

Then the Company was back, and once more the household in Moone Crescent was complete. Pelagia vividly described the delights and horrors of touring and made a good story of the night when she had had hiccoughs, but mostly she was quieter than usual, drifting round the house like a thin, red-haired ghost or playing sad music on her record-player.

"I believe she's missing Timothy," said Anne, perhaps made more aware because of her own experience with Lisa. Pelagia was proud and might never ask Timothy to come back, but where was Timothy himself? There were times when Anne almost telephoned him to tell him that he was silly to stay away, but she always decided not to interfere.

"Why on earth did you ditch Timothy?" asked Delphine, who felt that she could say anything these days. She had been very much spoilt since her accident, and, though it was possible that the "death-bed conversion" might show some results when she returned to the Thorburg School next term, there was certainly little sign of Saint Delphine.

Pelagia glared.

"Mind your own business! In any case, you *know* why I ditched him. Because I didn't want to get married and he bothered so."

"Bet you miss him now, though."

"I haven't *time* to miss him," her sister said, with desperate calm. "I'm busy. I'm going to Paris and a lot of other places. Tim's out." But her voice lacked conviction.

However, she came home the next day in a state of genuine excitement and pleasure, and actually pounced on Joan when she returned first from school. Joan, much startled to be seized and more or less hauled into the house by the girl who was usually lying flat on her back in the late afternoon, took some moments to grasp what had happened.

"I'm in your ballet, Joan. I'm the farm girl's sister – Margaret's sister. Shelagh Sullavan is Margaret, but I'm thrilled to get anything. It's my first real solo role. I can't count Little Clara. I get a dance with the Prince, just briefly, and then with one of the Highlanders. But of course you know all about it."

Joan looked at her. It seemed unlikely and extraordinary that her second ballet was taking on life and reality in the rehearsal rooms and the Thorburg workshop.

"I don't really know anything about the dancing. But I'm so glad that you're Jennie!"

"Oh, by the way, Mr Thorburg says that you'd better call in at the rehearsal rooms on Saturday morning if you want to see the choreography. I told him you don't break up until just before Easter. You ought to see the dances grow. He has his own method. 'Try this! No, we'll forget that! Let me see so and so.' And gradually something grows the way he wants it to."

So Joan went and had the strange experience of seeing her ballet in embryo, but it was not unmixed pleasure because by then she was growing frightened as well as thrilled. Paris, even though the Company was going to quite a small theatre, and the dreaded critics and the danger of a flop: Joan had not lived with the Garlands for months without learning a good deal about the terrifying power of theatre critics.

The ballet looked so strangely unfinished, too, bearing almost no relation to what she had had in mind. The men and girls in tights and sweaters dancing in the bare, sunlit room could, by no stretch of the imagination, be looked on as Lancashire farming people, citizens of eighteenth-century Manchester or members of the Highland Army.

She crept away feeling both alarmed and depressed, but the depression didn't last long. Excitement took hold of her again, because, after all, she was to see Paris in the spring and there was always the chance that the ballet would be a success or at least not a hopeless failure.

In fact excitement was boiling up throughout the Garland household. The dreadful winter was really almost over, daffodils were out in the parks at last and Anne's favourite magnolia was covered with huge waxen blossoms. The wind still blew coldly, but they were convinced that it would be warmer in Paris.

Term finished for everyone and there was time for looking over clothes, making plans, starting the packing. For Mr and Mrs Garland and Pelagia it was to be a long trip, lasting for several weeks, and there was a lot to do. Pelagia, when free of rehearsals in the afternoons, vowed that she could concentrate best to very loud music, but the others nearly went mad when she insisted on having one of their several record-players on full blast in whatever part of the house she happened to be occupying. Failing records, she carried her radio from room to room, and, if criticized, she was more apt than usual to snap.

"It *must* be Timothy!" said Anne. "I can't think why he doesn't make her see sense. But perhaps *he's* seen sense and that's what's upsetting her."

Anne was looking forward to Paris as though it were going to be a kind of release, an escape into another world. She longed to be free in a foreign city and to forget the strains, tensions and worries of the winter. So when she learned that Mrs Thorburg and Lisa were accompanying the Thorburg to Paris for a few days she didn't know whether to be glad or sorry. The Thorburgs were to stay at the same hotel as the Garlands in the Rue de Rivoli.

"William Royal is staying there too, and Barbary Brown and her little sister," said Edward.

"Barbary's *little* sister? Why, she's fifteen!" cried Anne. "Haven't you ever seen her? She goes to the Dawstone Stage School."

"She said her little sister when I happened to speak to her," said Edward. "No, I didn't even know she *had* a sister."

"Well, she's perfectly lovely. Very dark, and such a nice girl. I met her once at a party."

The dress rehearsal for *Farewell, Manchester* (*Adieu, Manchester*, according to the French programme sent to Joan by Johann Thorburg), took place immediately after Easter, but Joan didn't go. Everyone tried to persuade her, but she said she would sooner wait and see it in Paris, when it would be too late to alter anything or have any regrets.

Edwin Garland was conducting the orchestra and Mona Garland went to the rehearsal to watch Joan's ballet and one of the new Thorburg ballets in which she was not dancing. As a vehicle for Mona herself they were taking the ever-popular second act of *Swan Lake* and *Les Sylphides*, but the remainder of the ballets for a tour that was mostly planned for the smaller theatres were all short and many of them new.

She came back to reassure Joan, who had spent the morning working off some of her energy with Margaret and Bonne-Bouche in the park.

"I think it comes off, Joan dear. You used the procession idea very well in your first ballet and now you've brought off a similar thing with the Jacobite Army. It nearly made me cry when they marched off so triumphantly from Manchester, not knowing they were going to disaster. You're a clever, clever girl and your mother would have been proud of you."

"She didn't like the ballet," said Joan brusquely.

"She'd have been pleased, all the same. It's quite a remarkable achievement for a girl of fourteen. You should have been there to see it."

"I'll see it in Paris."

The scenery and costumes went off to France and most members of the Company and orchestra flew from London to Paris. The Garlands and Joan went by the short Channel crossing, because Mona Garland said that Joan would see more that way and it was always a pity to fly anywhere on a first visit.

By the time they were all sitting in the train at Victoria Joan was in such a state of suppressed excitement that she could hardly remain still, and Delphine *didn't* sit still, but wandered restlessly about, doing arabesques wherever there was space and generally behaving in a conspicuous way.

Anne was just going to tell her off sharply when she remembered the tragic Delphine who had thought she wouldn't dance again, and she thought that perhaps she ought to be glad that her sister could do an arabesque after all. All the same it was embarrassing to have people stare and murmur to each other that those must be the Garland children.

They sped through the blossoming orchards of Kent, and the Channel, when they came in sight of it, looked quite calm and blue, though the wind was still cold. The boat was not very crowded and the young ones spent most of the time on deck.

"I hope your French is good!" Anne teased, as Calais drew nearer and nearer, and Joan stared at the quays and the waiting, blue-clad porters with a wild thrill of excitement.

"I don't think my French is bad," she said tentatively. "And, by studying the street map and that old Métro map Uncle Edwin found for me, I think I can go anywhere. I most want to go to Montmartre to see all those little streets and squares that Utrillo painted. And the long flights of steps and lovely flinty walls. Utrillo and lots of others."

"Well, you can go where you like. Father and Mother won't fuss. They take it for granted that we're sensible in cities. And you manage fine in London."

Joan fully intended to "manage fine" in Paris, but was not quite prepared for the flood of rapid French that poured over her as the porters came on board. Still, she had once heard a seasoned traveller who knew few languages say that the best way to tackle a foreign city was to walk around confidently, saying as little as possible, then you soon sank into the landscape. Joan fully intended to try it and see if she could be taken for a French girl.

On the way to Paris the April countryside was lovely; the soft green of woodlands, blossoming orchards, and a sky that was certainly bluer than anything they had enjoyed for a long time in London made them all hope that it was going to be really warm in Paris. When they stopped at Amiens and Joan and Anne leaned out side by side, the air certainly seemed soft and the sun almost hot, and Joan listened again to the French voices. She smelt the subtle "foreign" fragrance of the train and once more could hardly believe in her good fortune.

Only Pelagia seemed in low spirits and scarcely moved from her corner seat. She looked very charming in a new green suit, with a matching top coat and a little green hat made almost entirely of feathers; she had her solo role and was going to Spain, so she should have been happy. She pretended that she had a headache, but really it was a strange, nagging heartache because it was now so many weeks since the parting from Timothy. And now he had let her leave England without a single word, or even a bunch of flowers to show that he was still thinking of her and missed her. Perhaps he *didn't* miss her ... Pelagia got almost no thrill from her first glimpse of the Sacré-Coeur on the Butte de Montmartre because that idea hurt so surprisingly.

Pelagia drove away alone from the Gare du Nord, because she had insisted on staying with the other members of the *corps de ballet* in a small hotel on the Left Bank. The rest of the family divided themselves and all the luggage into two taxis and they sped through the bright early evening, through streets that were greyer than Joan had expected. But her long studying of the map had served her well, for she knew just where they were going and she was not surprised – though she was certainly thrilled – when they swept round the Opera House and she saw the impressive frontage, with its stone balustrades and flags, and the whole big stretch of the Place de l'Opéra and the Avenue de l'Opéra.

"L'Opéra's *much* more impressive than Covent Garden!" she cried, as the taxi shot towards the Rue de la Paix and the grave, symmetrical beauty of the Place Vendôme beyond.

"Only because you can see it properly," Anne said quickly. "If you could stand away from Covent Garden it would look good, too. Oh, Paris in the spring! *Look* at the Tuileries Gardens, Mother. all that heavenly pale green. When can we walk along the Champs-Elysées?"

"Tonight you'll just unpack, have a meal and go to bed."

At that all the younger ones set up a wail and the taxi driver turned round and cocked an eye at them, quite regardless of the fact that he was driving along the Rue de Rivoli in a stream of traffic.

"That, of course, doesn't apply to me," said Edward grandly.

"Then it doesn't to us, either," Delphine insisted. "Why, we have to see the theatre, and I heard Joan saying she wants to go to Montmartre, and *I'd* like to go up the Eiffel Tower just as soon as possible. I haven't been here since I was seven, remember, and that was really too young to enjoy it to the full."

However, the argument wasn't continued then for they had reached their hotel. And there, in the entrance hall, were William Royal, Barbary Brown – looking wonderful in a white suit – and with Barbary was a beautiful little dark girl, who stared shyly at the new arrivals.

"My little sister, Leonora," said Barbary, to anyone who was listening, and Edward certainly was. In all the weeks since he had parted from Tarn in a snowstorm he had scarcely looked at a girl, but now he looked at Leonora and smiled, and Leonora smiled back, shyly but warmly. Joan saw it with a slight lessening of pleasure; she had been hoping that perhaps Edward might go around with her a little in Paris. Now she told herself that she had been an idiot to imagine anything of the kind. Edward seemed to have accepted her as another sister and that was the end of it.

"Ed's settled, I think," remarked Anne, as she and Joan

stood at the window of the room they were to share, looking down at the roaring traffic and across the road to the Tuileries Gardens, with a glimpse of the Louvre to the left. "Did you see how he looked at Leonora Brown? Well, she's nice; not like Tarn Marlow. And Ed speaks good French, so he'll look after her."

Joan made no reply for a moment, then said, "I can't, can't believe that we're really in Paris! If only it wasn't for my ballet ... I'm getting dreadfully scared –"

"It'll be all right," said Anne kindly. She could, she felt, afford to be nice to Joan now that they were away from London, though of course it was going to be awful if Joan and Lisa ganged up and left her alone, or just with Delphine.

"I'm being silly," she told herself. "I expect we'll all go together and I must behave properly. We *could* all three be friends."

But a wave of sadness went through her because there was still a barrier between herself and Lisa and might be for ever more. In Paris, in the springtime, one ought to be happy.

So, too, Pelagia was thinking as she settled into the hotel on the Left Bank. She could just glimpse the towers of Notre-Dame and one of the glorious rose windows from her high room among the roof-tops, and if she stood on tip-toe she could see the delicate spire of Sainte Chapelle to the left. A little more effort and there was the pale, heart-stirring green of the trees along the Seine. In Paris, thought Pelagia, one ought to be in love. Yet probably, by now, Timothy had found another girl.

It seemed to Pelagia then, as she began to stow away her clothes behind the spotlessly clean curtain that did duty as a wardrobe, that even the Spanish sun wouldn't be able to cure her unhappiness. As for the shimmering leaves of Paris ... the warm promise of the air ... Pelagia felt some reluctance to go out and sit at a pavement restaurant with other members of the *corps de ballet.* It was a long time since she had been treasured and looked at with adoration and now she wanted it desperately. But only from one person. And that one person was far away. For a crazy moment Pelagia wondered how much it would cost to telephone Timothy in London, but pride got the better of her and everyone thought how cheerful she was as they went out to look for a meal in the Boulevard Saint Michel.

Chapter Fourteen
A Happy Ending?

The Thorburgs were there when the Garlands went down for dinner and Lisa looked very pretty in a new cherry-red dress. But, though they all had coffee together afterwards – except Edward, who had his with Leonora Brown – there was not much chance to talk. Mona Garland was as good as her word and insisted that Anne, Joan and Delphine should go to bed, because it was already quite late and they had none of them slept much the night before. Lisa, whose room was just along the corridor, came to see Anne and Joan briefly and they agreed that it was wonderful to be in Paris in the spring.

The Rue de Rivoli was noisy, but Anne slept almost at once, and when she awoke it was seven o'clock, with sunlight shining brilliantly into the room.

"Paris!" thought Anne. She slipped out of bed and ran to the window, dazzled by the morning light and the soft blaze of green. But after a moment she recognized a figure crossing the road during a pause in the traffic. The figure was showing due respect for Parisian drivers by running, and Anne laughed softly, for she always felt the same temptation. Even when the traffic lights told you sternly to "walk" running seemed the safest, especially on the wide avenues.

Anyway, as she watched Lisa gained the opposite pavement and turned towards one of the entrances to the Tuileries Garden. Lisa was making the best of the lovely April morning, and, almost without thinking, Anne began quietly and swiftly to dress, glancing occasionally at Joan, who was more or less buried under the bedclothes. Anne didn't want Joan; she wanted to go out alone into the bright morning to find Lisa.

Five minutes later she was walking through the still quiet hotel. The only people about were young chambermaids, who were applying some of the sweet-smelling polish to the pale wood, and they smiled at her and said, "*Bonjour, Mademoiselle*!" Anne said "*Bonjour*!" in reply and hurried on through the entrance hall, where the night porter looked sleepy and eager for the end of his vigil, and out into the roar and glitter of the Rue de Rivoli.

But once she entered the gardens the roar immediately seemed far away and the sunlight glimmered and sparkled through the young leaves. Anne wore flat sandals, so the yellow gravel so beloved of the French did not really bother her, and she set off briskly towards the main avenue. When she reached it she paused to stare about her, almost forgetting Lisa.

The broad, beautiful avenue gave views one way of the Carrousel Arch and the vast buildings of the Louvre, and westwards to the obelisk and statues in the Place de la Concorde, with the Arc de Triomphe looming up at the end of the Champs-Elysées. Nearer, at either end of the gardens, were round pools with fountains, and the April light lay over everything with an almost heart-stopping clarity.

Lisa's bright jacket showed up unmistakably. She was walking very slowly indeed towards the Place de la Concorde. Anne followed her, enjoying the sweet smells, happy as she had not been for many cold and depressing weeks. It was going to be all right; she had never been more sure of anything.

Lisa did not go straight out of the Tuileries Gardens into the Place de la Concorde, but climbed the slope that led to the Jeu de Paume and stood gazing at the vast square from the slight eminence. Her face lit up when Anne said "Hullo!" and she turned and saw her friend.

"Oh, Anne! What luck! I – I wanted to ask you to come, but I thought we'd have to have Joan, too, and you wouldn't like it. Isn't it a heavenly morning? And don't you adore Paris?"

Anne gazed reflectively at the point where the Rue Royale came in between two impressive blocks of pale buildings.

"I followed you. I saw you from my bedroom window. Isn't it strange, Lisa, to think that this is where most of them died during the Revolution? Life has gone on and it looks so busy and civilized, so truly Parisian. But they came here in all that terror. I was thinking about it coming through the gardens. Thinking of Marie Antoinette in the Conciergerie and –"

Lisa nodded, moving a little to gaze at the arcades at the beginning of the Rue de Rivoli.

"I wonder how different it was?"

"I read a book once that told about it. There was no Rue de Rivoli then. They came down the Rue Royale, between those same buildings and the guillotine was over there ... Lisa, I didn't mean to talk about the Revolution. Everything seems new this morning. The winter's gone and – and I want to say – look, I'm sorry. I've wanted to say it for a very long time. I was a beast, and I suppose I never understood, and you couldn't help getting friendly with Joan and Margaret. Only let *us* understand each other again. I've so dreadfully minded having to watch my words, when once I could say anything to you and you'd understand. No one else is like you, though Helenka is nice."

Lisa turned, putting her hand on Anne's arm, and they walked very slowly back towards the round pool, which was reflecting the morning sky.

"Oh, Anne, I've missed it, too! Joan and Peigi aren't the same. It isn't easy to build up the thing that we had. I hated it when everything went wrong and you wouldn't even mention ballet or the Thorburg."

"I thought it was safer not to."

"But I *wanted* you to talk about them. I didn't want to cut them right out of my life, just because I stopped intending to be a dancer. I *wanted* to hear all the gossip and feel I still belonged just a little through you. It wasn't the same just hearing things from Father. He doesn't know the gossipy things, anyway, that *we* find so interesting."

"I honestly thought you didn't care. That you were quite happy."

Lisa snorted.

"Well, that *was* silly of you. How could I be? I liked the Scott-Smithson, and I was glad that Joan and Peigi were so friendly, but I was very miserable about you. Only it got to the point when I thought it was hopeless and we'd never get right with each other."

"I don't believe it would have got so bad if it hadn't been for the beastly winter and –"

"Well, never mind. It's over now. Let's forget the whole thing and enjoy Paris. And next term tell me every single thing about the Thorburg and try and learn about the Scott-Smithson, eh?" Lisa gave her friend a bright, almost shy glance.

"I know quite a lot about the Scott-Smithson, actually. I will be better. I won't mind when you have jokes with Joan."

"*We'll* have jokes, too. There's no *need* to be jealous of Joan. The poor girl was only trying to be kind and helpful."

"I'm not now. I like Joan, really. She's terribly clever and awfully nice. We'd better take her and Delph out somewhere today. Ed has a new girl friend."

"Lee Brown? I know. I saw them last night. She'll be far better for Edward than that awful Tarn Marlow. Lee may go to a stage school, but she's very shy and I shouldn't think she's ever been out with a boy."

"Ed will show her Paris."

"And *we'll* show it to Joan and Delph."

"Joan probably knows it as well as I do," Anne remarked. "She's spent hours with books and maps. Oh, I'm starving!"

"Well, let's go and have coffee and rolls at the first place we come to in the Rue de Rivoli. I've got some French francs."

"*Le petit dejeuner*? How nice! But I haven't even washed my face, I was so afraid of waking Joan. But I did just wipe it over."

Lisa laughed and they walked cheerfully out of the Tuileries Gardens. Not a great deal had been said, but both knew that all would be well. The old strain and misunderstanding had been part of wintry London and had now ceased to exist in Paris in the spring.

The Company was rehearsing that morning, so Mona Garland was glad to have Delphine looked after by the older girls.

"Are you sure you've got plenty of francs? Take a taxi if you get lost or too tired."

"Oh, we'll use the Metro," Anne said, laughing. "Joan will insist. She hasn't learned every single station and *correspondance* for nothing."

"Joan isn't going to be really happy until after tomorrow evening," said that young lady grimly. "I wish my ballet was tonight. I wish there weren't any critics, because they're probably going to flay it, anyway. I wish I'd never done a second one. I wish –"

"Oh, pipe down!" Anne said, but she gave her cousin a warm smile to soften the words. "We'll all go to Montmartre. You'll forget all about your ballet when you see all those lovely little shabby squares and cobblestoned streets. And there won't be many trippers in April."

"Anne looks quite different," Mona Garland remarked, as she and her husband went to the theatre by taxi. "She went out early with Lisa, I gather, and they didn't come back until after breakfast."

"I wish Pelagia would perk up," Edwin Garland said. "She does seem unlike herself these days."

"She misses Timothy, of course, but I told him to stay away as long as he could. Maybe until she came back from this tour."

He gazed at her.

"You did? Good heavens! Why?"

"At the time it seemed the best advice. Then when I saw how she was in Scotland and the North I almost telephoned him to ask him to meet the train when we returned to London, but I decided it was up to him. I could have been wrong and then they'd have had it all to go through again. Now I hope to heaven he hasn't decided to give up."

Pelagia was going through the stage door just in front of them and laughing and talking, but her father was sure that she was even thinner than she used to be.

Pelagia herself knew it. She was several pounds lighter and it was all Timothy's fault. But of course he wasn't coming back and *she* certainly wasn't going to ask him to.... She tried to lose herself in the important rehearsal, ready for the opening that night, but when it was over she slipped away alone, crossing the Place du Châtelet and then one of the Seine bridges to walk on the Ile de la Cité.

Presently she descended some steps to be nearer the river; delicate leaves spilled down the golden-grey walls above her and, out of the wind, the sun was very warm. Pelagia strolled and stopped and strolled again, very near the water, and none of the young Frenchmen who noticed and admired her dared to do anything about it because she was followed so purposefully by a young man, probably English, who never took his eyes off her slender back and shining red hair.

Perhaps Pelagia felt eyes on her back, at all events she suddenly looked over her shoulder, cried "*Tim!*", caught her foot against a stone and fell with an enormous splash into the Seine.

Pretty girls don't fall into the River Seine at all regularly and it was immediately a challenge to every young man in sight. Frenchmen came running, but Timothy, being nearest, was first. He stood on the bank, kicking off his shoes and frantically unbuttoning his jacket. An English tourist – a fat woman in very high heels – cried shrilly: "She's drowning! Someone do something!" and *a bateau mouche* crowded with sightseers stopped in mid-stream and a sailor was seen coiling a rope.

Pelagia, rising like Ondine, with her hair dark and flattened with water, called sharply: "Tim, don't be a idiot! I can swim!"

Timothy, only half-believing her, stopped unbuttoning his jacket and, in his stockinged feet, bent down to grab her hand. Several of the young Frenchmen promptly joined him, jostling politely for the other hand, and Pelagia was heaved out of the water, dripping, coughing and (to Timothy and possibly everyone else) perfectly beautiful in spite of it. She seemed even more beautiful when she flung herself into Timothy's arms and cried: "I've missed you so much! Oh, Tim, I'm so glad you've come!"

Timothy was, however, enough of an Englishman to feel

that this was overdoing things in public, even though it was so delightful, so he disentangled her gently, tried to get into his shoes with as much dignity as possible, and said: "Heavens! You are wet, love! We'd better find a taxi quickly."

The *bateau mouche* went on its way, the Frenchmen dispersed, with regret, and Timothy led his love up to the road above and thrust her into the first taxi that came along, to the intense curiosity of the driver. He hoped that there hadn't been a quarrel and that she had been trying – or pretending – to commit suicide. Not that he really believed the calm English to be capable of such abandoned behaviour.

Pelagia, causing much interest in the entrance hall of the hotel as she passed, went to her room, had a bath and washed her hair – the Seine was certainly not very clean – and emerged looking a trifle damp still, but very pretty. She and Timothy then had an extremely late lunch and afterwards walked under the chestnuts (not in flower, but ready to burst out any minute) in the Champs-Elysées, and by the time Anne, Lisa, Joan and Delphine returned from a wholly satisfying day exploring Paris, they were happily engaged and even planning the wedding.

"In the autumn, we think," said Pelagia, "about a month after I get back from America. And you can all be bridesmaids. Yes, you, too, Lisa, if you like. Oh, it's wonderful to get things settled!"

The others gazed at her almost speechlessly, but she gave them little time to ask questions. She had to whirl away to get ready to go to the theatre.

"And it'll always be like that," said Anne. "She'll always be dashing off somewhere, Tim. But oh! I *am* glad!"

Timothy was glad too. It seemed a year since that morning, when he had followed Pelagia from the theatre. It certainly *was* wonderful to have things settled.

The next morning Joan said she had to go out by herself. For one thing she was extremely unsettled, and for another she felt that she couldn't really savour Paris until she had explored it alone. So she put on one of her nicest dresses, and, wearing prim white gloves, sallied forth to put the seasoned traveller's theory to the test. She walked very briskly along the Rue de Rivoli, not idling like a tourist, and presently her feet took her to the theatre near the Place du Châtelet. And there, on the placards, her ballet was advertised.

If *only*, thought Joan, the evening was over, and little curls of excitement ran up her spine and made her hair-roots tingle; excitement and dread. She was still standing there when Johann Thorburg came along and greeted her warmly.

"Hullo, Joan, my dear! Are you looking forward to tonight?"

"No, Mr Thorburg, not really. I'm dreadfully frightened. You see, I know now that *The Procession Passes* wasn't important. But this – this is really something that has to succeed in the commercial theatre. And I feel awful, and really I wish I hadn't done it, and if the critics are unkind about my designs I'll – I'll curl up and die."

He took her arm gently and led her to the nearest café, where he made her sit at a table on the pavement and ordered coffee.

"It's always frightening," he said, when the coffee had been put in front of them. "Make no mistake about it. It's my ballet, too, remember, and your uncle's. It's always an adventure and a challenge to put on anything new, and perhaps even more so in a foreign country."

"Oh, of course I know that only a little bit of it was mine."

"I didn't mean that. There would have been no *Adieu, Manchester* without you. But ballets are always to some

extent communal efforts. Now listen to me, my dear. Tonight you'll come to the theatre and you'll watch and listen and you'll probably know whether or not the audience likes it. You will *not* know whether the critics do until you read their pieces in the newspapers tomorrow morning. But whatever they say you must not curl up and die; how foolish that would be. If you are to get anywhere – and the same would apply to some extent if you were writing books or painting pictures – you must learn to bear criticism, and criticism that often seems unfair, and go on to the next thing. I don't wish to preach, but that's the first hard lesson."

Joan saw the kindly concern in his eyes and knew that he was really trying to help her. And she appreciated it very much, because he was an important man and very busy.

"I know you're right, Mr Thorburg. I've heard all the Garlands talking and Aunt Mona has a special press clipping book for all her unfavourable notices. Some of them when she was young were just dreadful, but she went on in spite of it to become a great ballerina. I *will* bear it and not give up."

"There may be nothing to bear," he said, smiling. "But I should be prepared for some adverse criticism. There may be some praise, too, as critics rarely agreed. Sometimes they seem to have seen a different ballet."

These words stayed with Joan all day, somewhere at the back of her mind, and when evening came she ran upstairs to dress, feeling, now that the moment had almost arrived, that it *was* exciting.

A block of seats at the front of the Circle had been reserved for the Garlands, Joan, Mrs Thorburg and Lisa, and Joan gazed around the pretty little theatre, aware of the French people all about her. A feeling of being in a dream had now descended on her. This was Paris! And soon the curtain would go up, though not, at first, to reveal the Scottish Royal Standard, for one of the other new ballets came first.

The audience really seemed warmly disposed towards the Company and the first ballet was received so well that Anne squeezed Joan's hand reassuringly.

"It will be all right. You'll see."

And then the overture that Edwin Garland had devised began to sound through the darkened theatre and the strange miracle happened. The curtain rose to reveal the Standard, and then, as the overture came to an end, the stark view of the Northern hills. And Joan was lost, sitting tense and rather cold in the warm auditorium.

For a long time, as she watched, the ballet might have had nothing to do with her, might not have been conceived long ago in Lancashire, when her mother was alive and the Garlands only a name to her.

First the farm people danced and there was Pelagia as the young girl, Jennie, with her red hair loose and flying, and then a messenger arrived with the news that the Prince and his army were approaching. And in they came, to wild, stirring music that very cleverly suggested bagpipes, banners waving, short kilts swinging. The people about Joan made little sounds of appreciation and some of them clapped. But still it was not Joan's ballet, even though her name was on the programme.

Some of the Lancashire men, including Margaret's and Jennie's own brother, decided to join the Prince's army, and when they marched away south to Manchester Margaret herself insisted on going, too, to be with her Highland love for as long as possible. They marched away, leaving Jennie, a little sadly, to dance alone, and the curtain came down briefly, rising again to reveal the city backcloth.

It was in this scene that the dancing took on real fire and sparkle, for the Prince and his men were sure of victory when they reached London. Margaret and her Highlander had a long *pas de deux* after their wedding, and the Prince danced with some of the local girls. Then it was time to go; time to go on with the adventure, the bold attempt to seize the crown. And once more the men formed up, the banners waved for the last time, and to the sound of *Farewell, Manchester* they gradually disappeared.

And, watching then, Joan suddenly flared into full awareness, realizing, as she had done in the Thorburg Theatre before Christmas, the strange thrill of creation. Whatever the critics said in the morning she would have to continue, would have to try again and again to create something worthwhile.

The Royal Standard descended slowly from the flies, an enormous affair that almost hid the Manchester backcloth, and the music grew wilder and wilder, at first exciting and then changing gradually to a lament that sobbed through the theatre. Then Margaret was there alone, dancing quietly, and finally a Highland messenger came to tell her that her husband was dead. Slowly, slowly she danced as the curtain came down, and Joan found herself gripping Anne's hand, with the tears unashamedly pouring down her cheeks.

The applause was warm, even very enthusiastic, but Joan scarcely heard. She was fighting for composure, for she had suddenly remembered her unemotional mother and what she would have said if she had seen her daughter crying in public. But it was a French theatre, and no one seemed to have noticed, in any case.

"I thought it was marvellous, really," said Anne. "Some of those Scottish dances were grand, and it was so exciting when they marched away from Manchester. And Pel was very good; it was a nice little role."

Joan still felt so dazed that she scarcely noticed what was happening, and by the time she came fully to herself she was in a taxi with Anne, Delphine and Lisa.

"But where are we going?" she cried, as they sped up a long hill.

Anne laughed.

"Wake up! Didn't you hear Father and Mrs Thorburg saying we'd better finish the evening by going up to the terrace in front of the Sacré-Coeur? Father said we ought to see Paris from up there at night and you'd never sleep, anyway, if you went to bed straight away. Father and Mother and Mrs Thorburg are in another taxi, and I think Pel and Tim are somewhere about, too."

"No, I couldn't have slept," Joan agreed, as they came up into the narrow little cobbled streets of the Butte de Montmartre. They went slowly along the Rue Norvins, through the Place du Tertre, where, though it was growing late, people were still sitting at gaily-clothed tables under the trees, and swung round on to the high terrace in front of the great white, floodlit Basilica of the Sacré-Coeur.

They all scrambled out, realizing that the other two taxis were just behind, and Joan gasped to see Paris outspread far below. The night was warm and the moon was almost at the full, and she moved a little way away from the others, leaning on the stone balustrade above the long flights of white steps, gazing at the half-seen city.

"Paris, and I am here!" Joan said to herself. "Paris, and they've done my ballet, and I don't care – no, I really don't, at the moment – what the critics say in the morning. Except that I should be dreadfully sorry and ashamed if the Thorburg lost money on it."

But there seemed no danger of that, with the theatre almost fully booked for the whole of their stay.

Presently Joan looked round for the others and saw Pelagia and Timothy quite near her; Timothy had his arm round Pelagia's waist and they were gazing down at Paris, apparently perfectly happy. Anne and Lisa were together, and Delphine – well, Delphine was doing a characteristic thing. She was executing a little dance in the middle of the pavement.

"For heaven's sake, Delph!" Anne's voice came clearly. "We're not alone. What will people think?"

"It's called *Salute to Paris Under the Moon*," her sister said complacently. "So I'm a choreographer, too. And people *like* it."

Joan laughed softly to herself and turned again to the view below, after one glance at that vast church looming behind her. The future might bring other worries and problems, but just now nothing mattered but being in Paris on a lovely night.

"I never knew I could be so happy," Joan said to herself, and she began to stroll towards Anne and Lisa, for she did not think that Anne resented her now.